Great Big Agile

An OS for Agile Leaders

Jeff Dalton

Apress®

Great Big Agile: An OS for Agile Leaders

Jeff Dalton
Waterford, MI, USA

ISBN-13 (pbk): 978-1-4842-4205-6
https://doi.org/10.1007/978-1-4842-4206-3

ISBN-13 (electronic): 978-1-4842-4206-3

Library of Congress Control Number: 2018965605

Managing Director, Apress Media LLC: Welmoed Spahr
Acquisitions Editor: Susan McDermott
Development Editor: Laura Berendson
Coordinating Editor: Rita Fernando

Cover designed by eStudioCalamar

Cover image designed by Freepik (www.freepik.com)

Distributed to the book trade worldwide by Springer Science+Business Media New York, 233 Spring Street, 6th Floor, New York, NY 10013. Phone 1-800-SPRINGER, fax (201) 348-4505, e-mail orders-ny@springer-sbm.com, or visit www.springeronline.com. Apress Media, LLC is a California LLC and the sole member (owner) is Springer Science + Business Media Finance Inc (SSBM Finance Inc). SSBM Finance Inc is a **Delaware** corporation.

For information on translations, please e-mail rights@apress.com, or visit http://www.apress.com/rights-permissions.

Apress titles may be purchased in bulk for academic, corporate, or promotional use. eBook versions and licenses are also available for most titles. For more information, reference our Print and eBook Bulk Sales web page at http://www.apress.com/bulk-sales.

Any source code or other supplementary material referenced by the author in this book is available to readers on GitHub via the book's product page, located at www.apress.com/9781484242056. For more detailed information, please visit http://www.apress.com/source-code.

Printed on acid-free paper

To my lovely wife Patricia.
"I think I'll write a book about that."

Table of Contents

About the Author

Jeff Dalton thinks the future of Big Agile is our industry's biggest challenge, and he has been studying it for years. As the large adopters in the federal government and corporate sector begin to adopt agile, they will bring their habits, culture, and bureaucracies with them; and in dozens of podcasts, articles, books, and keynote speeches, Jeff has been talking about getting in front of the wave. A veteran technologist and IT leader, Jeff started as a software developer and has been a CEO, chief technology executive, vice president of product development, director of quality, and Agile evangelist for over 30 years, including time with Ernst and Young, Electronic Data Systems, Hewlett Packard, Intellicorp, Polk, Broadsword, and AgileCxO. As a consultant, teacher, CMMI lead appraiser, and leadership coach, he has worked with NASA, Boeing, Accenture, Bose, L3 Communications, Fiat Chrysler Automotive, General Motors, Ford, and various federal and state agencies to help them improve performance. Jeff is a frequent keynote speaker, Agile performance holarchy assessor, blogger, and host of The Agile Leadership Podcast, a monthly series that interviews CIOs from state government about the challenges of agile adoption. In his spare time he is an instrument-rated pilot and plays bass in a jazz band.

About the Technical Reviewer

Michael Ogorek is a consultant with more than 30 years in information technology, manufacturing, and the automotive industry. His professional experience spans strategy and market planning, business development, and process improvement.

Mike uses proven capability models and agile frameworks to identify process improvement opportunities.

In the automotive sector, he has conducted more than 50 Supplier Design Capability Appraisals on behalf of a major automotive OEM. He has participated as a team member in CMMI appraisals and is a Certified Agile Performance Holarchy Coach, Instructor, and Assessor (AgileCxO.org). His website is OgorekAndAssociates.com.

In his spare time, Mike is a jazz musician and plays the vibes.

Foreword

Ever since the day that seventeen software development thought leaders wrote the Agile Manifesto in 2001, agile has caught the attention and imagination of the software development community. These seventeen pioneers sought a lightweight software development framework, and they proposed a set of values to support one, but published only the Agile Manifesto. They did not develop a new model or endorse an existing one. But they did lay down a marker with their core agile values. Then began the proliferation of models and frameworks that aligned with the Agile Manifesto, most focused on software development. However, in my own brush with the agile frameworks as implemented in organizations, I've found the common thread to be limited to the minimization of documentation.

Many software development organizations began adopting agile frameworks, such as scrum and Extreme Programming, but when attempting to scale, they needed more explanation and detail than the pioneers envisioned they would ever need. "Learning by doing" can be difficult at scale, although there are examples of successful agile implementations being practiced by software development organizations around the globe, with each organization enriching the model with their own flavor.

Now that many software development organizations are attempting to integrate both agile and established certification models such as ISO9000 and CMMI to derive the advantages from both, it's time to consider a new approach. Agile frameworks provide the nimbleness needed in the software development process, and models like CMMI give confidence to the prospective customers and management in the capability of the software development organizations as a whole. I have to acknowledge that there is a knowledge gap in the software development industry about marrying process-quality models with agile methodologies so that they can have their cake and eat it too. While there are a few books penned by different authors to bridge precisely this gap, I feel there still is a gap that needs bridging.

Who is better qualified to bridge this gap besides my good friend Jeff Dalton, who has been one of the few CMMI Lead Appraisers and Agile evangelists, besides being a consultant and leadership coach for so many great software development organizations? Thus, took birth, the idea for this book *Great Big Agile: an OS for Agile Leaders*. I was intrigued by the subject, especially the use of the word "Holarchy" throughout the book, an uncommon word that is not even in the dictionary! After some research I learned that it was a term that was first used in Arthur Koestler's book, *The Ghost in the Machine* (Penguin, 1967). Simply, it is a form of self-organizing hierarchy, but as you will see in this book, Jeff used this term and made it his own, building his model around this concept and giving us a fresh look at software development performance. Whether you are a leader, fan, adherent, or just a simple practitioner of any of the agile frameworks, this is a must-read for you. I enjoyed reading it and expanded my knowledge immensely. Jeff is a great writer of prose and I envy him for that quality! I am sure you will enjoy reading it while expanding your knowledge horizons at the same time. I recommend it heartily.

Murali Chemuturi
Software developer and author
Hyderabad, India
September 2018

Acknowledgments

Writing a book is harder than I thought, and I sure didn't do it alone! So many people contributed ideas, editing, logistics, management, and support that I can't possibly name them all. Some of them are:

My wife Patty, who diligently kept working while I paced and reacted to her editing of my work. I love you.

Sam Melroy, who provided the fabulous illustrations for this book. You are immensely talented, and your cheerful and enthusiastic spirit is a joy to work with. Thank you!

Michelle Rauch, who herded the cats and helped keep me focused on the schedule. I couldn't have done this without you!

Members of the Broadsword team who contributed research and content for some of these chapters, including Tim Zeller, Ross Timmeran, Darian Poinsetta, Cathy Henderson, Laura Adkins, Julie Calfin. You're the A-Team!

Members of the Broadsword team who provide logistical, marketing, and administrative support, including Amy Wilson, Rob MacDonald, and Patricia Dalton. Thank you!

The Apress team, who had faith and helped get me across the finish line. Special thanks to Rita Fernando Kim, my ever patient (and helpful) Coordinating Editor; and Susan McDermott, my Senior Editor, who never lost faith as I went through the process of deciding what I really wanted to write about.

My mother and father, who always knew that I'd write this book, and who will read it even though they don't know quite what I do.

Jacob and Dakota, my two sons, who make me work hard to maintain my "cool-dad-ness." How does this work for you?

Preface

I wasn't always a technologist. In fact, I was the furthest thing from it.

My childhood was a little different than most of my friends. By eight years old, I was touring in our family's music group, joining my parents and three siblings as the bassist for the Dalton Family Singers, a traditional American Folk Music group that performed up and down the North American eastern seaboard from 1968 to well into the 1980s. It was so "normal" for me that I used to ask my friends where their family was touring this summer! The "Singers" was my father's brainchild, who reasoned that a family music group was the perfect incubator for his musical children, and also an opportunity to practice and demonstrate to us the entrepreneurship required to run a successful entertainment franchise in a crowded market. Before the internet and Twitter, there was my Dad with his typewriter, press releases and corded phone.

Following those years I attended formal music school, first at the internationally recognized Interlochen Arts Academy, and then the Peabody Conservatory of Music in Baltimore (now part of Johns Hopkins University). I cut my studies short at Peabody to spend the next decade honing my craft as a concert double bassist with orchestras in Spain, Mexico, and the United States.

What did I learn during those years? Craftsmanship. Discipline. Collaboration. Transparency. Perfection. Persistence. Ceremony. Value. And also, how to self-subscribe and commit to excellence while working together with over one hundred other artists under the direction of a conductor to create some of the most sublime music known to mankind. It's a pretty good model for agility.

The other important thing I learned was the art of the retrospective. Not the standard retrospective we usually see in the typical agile teams, one of "what went well, what didn't, and what could we do better" with some people participating, and some grumbling a few perfunctory comments, but a comprehensive and sometimes brutal process that kept many music students up at night – known as "Juries." A CEO friend of mine, who also happens to be a musician and a visual artist himself, told me a story about his juries while attending art school in Pittsburgh. I recollect it went something like this:

> *Juries in Art school are brutal! They start right away during your freshman year don't stop until you're done. Both your teachers and fellow students critique your work in public, and most of them don't hold back! Those were tough times, but their real value is that you get used to the criticism, and your aversion to being evaluated melts away before long, letting you really focus on what's important – getting better! You also make sure that your next jury is as perfect as it can be!*

In the art world, where most of us aren't Mozart or Salvatore Dali, we know that the capability to be creative and innovative only comes after the hard work has been done. Not until the scales have been perfected, the arpeggios have been practiced until the fingers bleed, the concertos have been memorized, the music theory classes have been completed, and the performances have exceeded the prerequisite ten thousand hours, can we break the rules, experiment, and innovate at a world-class level. Only after we stop thinking about the *process* can we create something new, innovative, and exciting. Agile isn't any different. In many ways embracing agile requires the same commitment as a career in music or art –where rigor and discipline are paramount, not just the coding.

If this sounds like a systemic program to build a solid foundation for quality and early defect detection, while embracing a culture of excellence for continued high performance, it's because that's exactly what it is. In fact, trained musicians, artists, and dancers entering the technology workforce have a significant advantage over new engineers and software developers who don't have this experience –and it's the reason we often hear that "musicians make good coders." It's not because "music is math," by the way, it's the culture.

The first development team I ever led was building solutions for the international retail market, and we were creating the world's first touch-screen point-of-sale system. My second official act, after helping the team to establish much needed discipline around coding standards, was to implement "juries": public, collaborative, and transparent code reviews with the code projected larger than life on a ten-foot screen with the entire team in attendance. Team members were asked to present, and defend, their design and coding decisions. At first the team resisted with all their might –and who wouldn't? It was nerve wracking, uncomfortable, and stressful. But by the second month of doing weekly reviews, the code quality went up dramatically and the team went from combative and defensive individuals to an innovative, transparent, and collaborative team. This was 1994 – long before "agile" and values were in the headlines.

My journey from musician, to software engineer, to CEO has been one of many twists and turns, but the most important concept I've learned to harness along the way was "innovation lies on the far side of rigor." While we all believe ourselves to be innovative and creative, few of us are able to commit to the discipline to make ourselves world-class performers. But the proven lessons from music can help us get there.

This idea of foundational craftsmanship and relentless improvement found in the music industry can and should extend to the parallel universe of software development, where adoption of agile values and frameworks are akin to music theory and were designed specifically to foster innovation, experimentation, and continuous learning. So far this level of performance has mostly eluded very large organizations in the government and private sector who want to "go agile," but adoption of agile values along with an operating system for agile leadership can help.

But all is not well in the Land of Agile either. Many large adopters are struggling to achieve the results they expected, team members are often uncomfortable with the ambiguity inherent in agile projects, line managers don't know how to lead in high-trust self-organizing teams, and business customers complain that they have to spend too much time working on the project without getting the return on investment they were promised. In some cases, CIO's are finding it so complicated that they are now forbidding the use of Agile altogether! But, in every leading magazine, from *Harvard Business* Review to the *Cutter IT Business Journal* to *CIO*, and in every major survey, including Version One's "State of Agile Survey," we learn that the responsibility of these, and other issues related to limited success with large-scale agile adoption, rests squarely on the shoulders of leadership. My own observations from over two hundred agile assessments confirm this. While leaders are telling their teams to "be agile," they are not themselves adopting, practicing, and projecting agile values. This creates an *organizational type mismatch* where leaders are practicing their hard-earned *command-and-control* techniques, and teams are trying to self-organize in what is inevitably a *low-trust* environment. If you were a leader who spent their entire career learning to navigate in a low-trust environment, would you give it up that easily? This leads to chaos.

I am lucky enough in my work to collaborate with some of the greatest agile organizations in the world in my role as Chief Evangelist for AgileCxO.org, a research and development organization whose focus is on performance models and assessment methods for large agile organizations. Through that work I have observed that:

- Agile ceremonies often devolve into "water-scrum-fall" with scrum masters tasking team members, sprint durations changing based on workload, team members moving in and out of teams, and story points being normalized between teams as hours.

- Leaders continue to resist high-trust, self-organizing values.

- Product Owners are often "IT surrogates," negating the value of the business owning the risk and ROI of the product.

- Retrospectives are rarely conducted beyond the individual agile team community.

- Team members and leaders are not sufficiently trained in the rigor and discipline of agile ceremonies.

- Leader don't know what "agile looks like," and are unable to verify that teams are embracing agile values, ceremonies, and techniques in a way that makes sense for the business.

- Traditional, often punitive metrics are still being used, adding little value to the organization.

- Teams and leaders often "experiment" their way into chaos by eliminating or severely distorting the intention of the ceremony or technique they are using.

I was inspired to write this book while thinking of my experience as a professional musician, and how it informed and affected my own performance and thirty-year technology journey that started as software developer, and then rapidly moved to project manager, architect, Chief Technology Officer, Director of Product Development, VP of Global Consulting, CIO, and finally CEO of two of my own technology companies.

I wanted to provide agile leaders with those lessons in an illustrated guide that defines objectives, outcomes, and actions needed to successfully lead large-scale agile organizations. The resulting model, the Agile Performance Holarchy, is an implementation guide to bring solid Craftsmanship, Discipline, Collaboration, Transparency, Perfection, Persistence, Ceremony, and Value to your organization.

So join me in reviewing the scales, arpeggios, and concertos, and building a foundation of discipline and rigor in order to establish a sustainable and high-performing agile organization.

This book is about my own journey to excellence – I hope it helps you too!

PART I

The Agile Performance Holarchy

CHAPTER 1

The API Is Broken

As the prolific and popular SPaMCAST podcaster Tom Cagley proclaimed during his keynote at the 2017 Agile Leadership Camp, "Values aren't really what matters; behavior matters." Cagley, who has interviewed more than five hundred technology leaders on his podcast series, hit the nail squarely on the head. Culture is usually derived from organizational values.

The behavior of team members, business stakeholders, partners, and leadership is all that matters, as it demonstrates real, as opposed to stated, culture. Too many companies say the words while demonstrating antipatterns that proliferate throughout the organization. Instead, companies should project and promote behaviors that build scalable and sustainable self-organization at all levels.

While many leaders are asking about scaling agility these days, they are asking the wrong question. They should be asking how to scale self-organization supported by a healthy dose of agile values, frameworks, and techniques.

Throughout much of recorded history, people have lived and worked under a model I like to call "the rules of men." In this model, masses of people are organized into an elaborate command-and-control infrastructure to meet the goals of their leaders, -think Alexander the Great, Caesar, and Napoleon. The masses saw little, if any, of the benefit, while a cadre of leaders made the important decisions and rewarded themselves well for it. It is a model that benefits the organizers without much input from the organized, and it more or less still exists today.

From time to time, people have made attempts to transition from the "rules of men" to the "rules of nature," a system that more closely mimics the natural world. This is where the scales are inverted, roles and accountabilities are dispersed throughout the organization, and people go about the sometimes messy process of organizing themselves without having to ask permission from any business leader. Some of the

© Jeff Dalton 2019
J. Dalton, *Great Big Agile*, https://doi.org/10.1007/978-1-4842-4206-3_1

most famous examples of this include the American Revolution, the French Revolution (perhaps the messiest of all), and the agile movement within the technology industry. These revolutions created a clash of culture, where one side is governed by the laws of men; and the other side is modeled after the natural world, based on what we now call agile values.

According to a 2016 Gallup study, people's faith in traditional command-and-control institutions, specifically politics, media, banking, education, and Congress, has been steadily declining annually since the survey began asking these questions in 1973.[1] Yet, these same operating models are still pervasive in the technology industry today. It's no wonder that an "agile transformation" is so difficult!

In almost all of the over one hundred organizations we've assessed, tech leaders tell us that they want to push decision making down and give their teams greater autonomy, but the behaviors they demonstrate are in conflict with agile values, creating an *organizational type mismatch*. In other words, the API is broken, and the architecture needs to change.

Introducing Great Big Agile

What should Great Big Agile look like? This is our industry's most urgent challenge.

As the large adopters in the federal government and corporate sector begin to adopt agile, they will inevitably bring their habits, culture, and bureaucracies with them, creating their own brand of "CAGILE" (corporate agile) – and no one really wants to see that. Indeed, the same thing happened with "waterfall," and the use of models like CMMI and ISO. While not intended to be "heavy" and bureaucratic, these methods were adopted by large, complex organizations that already were process heavy, and they simply applied that culture to those methods and models as well. In the early days of Agile, small organizations, or small teams within larger organizations, were where the real growth was occurring. While many, if not most, small software organizations adopted agile early, large companies have been predictably slow to change, but that is no longer the case. Organizations as large as the Department of Defense, Health and Human Services, and General Motors are all actively exploring or "going agile," and the potential for dramatic change to the state of agile is high. Like "waterfall" before it, agile will change – unless we get in front of it now.

---

[1] Gallup Organization Survey 1973–2016.

By definition, leadership at these large adopters is likely to be "low-trust," "command-and-control," and process-heavy, and even though they are asking their teams to "be agile," they themselves, as a culture are not. Since Agile isn't a method, framework, or process, but a philosophical approach to collaboration and working that is based on a collective agreement on values, the results don't look promising. Without leadership buy-in, the value of agile is lost, and with the sheer size, budget, and influence that these organizations possess (the DOD spends over ten billion dollars a year on information technology), the result will be a continued low-trust environment while teams struggle to succeed by simply executing a few of the agile ceremonies.

The concept of "Great Big Agile" requires leadership at all levels, but just not the kind we are used to. Simply working with an agile coach to implement well-known ceremonies is not enough. Metaphorically, the operating system needs an upgrade.

In today's corporate hierarchies where command-and-control structures, low-trust, long-term planning, and risk management reign supreme, the skills required to thrive and survive are anything but agile. This leaves agile teams to push the culture uphill, leading to unpredictable results once business operations expand beyond the boundaries of the core agile team. This creates chaos because information technology, operations, marketing, infrastructure, business development, sales, and end users are not on the same page.

Agile without self-organization isn't agile at all. There is nothing wrong with adopting ceremonies and techniques that are most commonly identified as being agile, and many companies have found some success with that, but the power of agile values and their associated frameworks grows exponentially once self-organization is perfected.

How Agile Is Your Organization?

I have witnessed only a few examples of large organizations that have been successful with true agility, with far more insisting they are agile but merely adopting a couple of techniques or ceremonies within an otherwise command-and-control, low-trust, and traditional operating model.

When I first start an assessment, I interview the leadership at all levels to get some feel for the culture. Here are some comments from actual management interviews:

- Sure, we're agile, but why do we have to bother the customer?

- IT knows the customer's business; can't I just be the product owner?

- I want to adopt Scrum, but I need my MS Project work plan.

- Why do we have to meet every day? How about twice a week?

- Pair programming doubles our cost. Why spend the money?

- Why should we pay for automated build tools?

Even with impediments to self-organization and agility, companies and government agencies are increasingly turning to agile frameworks because they sense, correctly, that by improving their methods and tools, they may increase customer satisfaction, speed delivery of value, and raise the quality of software, systems and services. The problem is, they often think that it's *only* about changing their methods and tools, and they give short shrift to the power of culture.

Once the domain of mid-size software companies, "agile-like," a term that describes an organization that adopts some agile ceremonies without the accompanying organizational change, has become mainstream in the IT shops of Fortune 100 companies and government agencies.

Why Agile Matters

One hundred percent of the organizations I work with have expressed an interest in "going agile," if they have not already done so. This is a strategic decision that has deep-rooted cultural implications and should not be taken lightly. Many leaders do not realize the extent to which they have to change the way *they* behave.

There are several reasons why an organization should transition to a model that is agile and self-organizing:

Agile frameworks reduce the cost of failure. It is conventional wisdom in the technology industry that failure is inevitable, with many companies seeing failure rates greater than fifty percent.[2] Research conducted by organizations such as the Project Management Institute and the Software Engineering Institute has consistently confirmed high failure rates, so it makes sense to seek solutions that assume a low level of early failure, and to simply reduce its cost.

---

[2]IAG Consulting. The Impact of Business Requirements on the Success of Technology Projects.
https://www.zdnet.com/article/study-68-percent-of-it-projects-fail/
CIO Magazine: "More than half of IT projects still failing," May 11, 2016.

Failure is not just an option; it should be expected. A foundational premise of agile is the acknowledgment that early failure is normal, and we should plan to fail fast and learn as much as we can. This reduces a project's cost while allowing teams to redirect efforts toward a more successful approach through the use of experimentation, retrospectives, and short, timeboxed iterations. Quality professionals will recognize this as an application of W. Edwards Deming's "plan-do-check-act" framework of continuous improvement applied in short iterations.[3]

Agile methods deliver business value to end users more quickly. Value is delivered more quickly with an iterative and incremental delivery approach due to low-value features being de-prioritized or discarded, freeing up valuable resources to focus on the high-priority needs of the customer.

Self-organization pushes decision making downward, freeing leaders to focus on strategy. For decades, the technology industry has explored ways to push decisions downward. Agile frameworks finally provide a model that can make that a reality, if only leaders are willing to accept their role as enablers rather than task managers. A successful agile team requires minimal oversight, makes day-to-day operational decisions, collaborates with business customers, and delivers business value without the need for continuous management intervention.

Agile complements important IT industry models. Many say that CMMI, ISO 9001, and the PMBOK Guide are models we *use*, but agile is something we *are*. For example, the CMMI has a perspective of defining *what* needs to occur for a product or service to be successfully delivered, while agile values describe *why* we take those actions. If adopted in this way, CMMI can make agile stronger.[4] In the case of agile, which is best defined as a set of values and behavioral principles, the *why* modifies the *what* and subsequently results in behaviors and processes that are transparent, collaborative, and focused on delivering business value, as opposed to the documentation and process deliverables that are often perceived to be associated with the industry models.

---

[3]Deming, W. Edwards. *Out of Crisis*. Cambridge, MA: MIT Press, 2000.
[4]Dalton, Jeffrey. *The Guide to Scrum and CMMI – Making Agile Stronger with CMMI*. CMMI Institute, 2016.

All Is Not Well with Agile

While the popularity of agile frameworks like Scrum, Extreme Programming, and Scaled Agile Framework cannot be understated, in some ways, they have been a victim of their own success.

Large companies eager to replicate small company successes; satisfy younger, more self-organizing employees; and to just simply "go agile" have jumped on the agile bandwagon. Unfortunately, they often give inadequate attention to the changes in governance, infrastructure, measurement, and training required to succeed. The results have been chaotic, with large organizations adopting some elements of Scrum (e.g., daily standups and sprints) and force-fitting them with more traditional roles and techniques that are in conflict with agile values. This conflict dilutes the value of the very agile ceremonies they use and leaves the organization without the benefits they were hoping to achieve.

Here at AgileCxO, a research and development organization, we sponsor an observation-based organizational assessment and certification program designed to verify that the selected governance, frameworks, ceremonies, techniques, and values are aligned in a way that enables large-scale self-organization and successful agility at scale. This values traceability is essential to successful agile.

AgileCxO's partners assessed more than two hundred companies between 2010 and 2017 with these results.[5]

Out of more than two hundred companies assessed by AgileCxO and its partners:

- More than 90 percent assigned project managers for task management, oversight, and control of agile teams.

- More than half did not conduct regular retrospectives.

- Almost half conflated story points with hours yet still considered velocity to be a reliable metric.

- Most made no changes to governance, infrastructure, or training to support agile adoption.

- Many senior leaders were unable to describe what behaviors were expected in order to achieve sustainable agility.

---

[5]Agile Performance Holarchy and CMMI assessment results performed by AgileCxO and Transformation Partners 2010–2018.

These obvious conflicts with agile values result in a scenario where leaders may desire agility but continue to apply low-trust, defined process-control models to run the business, when a high-trust, empirical process-control model is required for successful agility. This friction, often manifesting itself as "Scrummerfall" or "ScrumBut" ("we're agile, but..."), corrupts and degrades the very performance that agile leaders are seeking to achieve.

Jim Bouchard, author of *The Sensei Leader*, sums it up: "Don't even attempt to transform your organization until you can transform yourself."[6]

The Missing Layer in the Operating System

While the Agile Manifesto excels in describing *why* we do what we do, and industry frameworks and models describe *what* we need to accomplish, there is little guidance for leaders or teams on *how* to experience consistent success with self-organization and agility. This layer isn't a process, but a set of guiderails that helps leaders and team members recognize what large-scale agile looks like and provide the ability to recognize, evaluate, and improve agile performance. As I often tell conference audiences during my talks, "It's not magic. You just need to be able to recognize it."

To succeed with "great big agile," technology leaders and teams can start by categorizing capability into three interdependent layers: *why*, *what*, and *how*.

"Why" models: The set of values and guiding principles that are traced directly to the goals and methods of the organization. With its guiding principles, the Agile Manifesto is perhaps the best example.

"What" models: The set of frameworks, methods, roles, and artifacts derived from industry-standard models or internal methodologies. These models define what needs to be done and often provide examples that help us understand what we need to do while executing the software product development process.

"How" models: A set of behaviors, actions, and outcomes that helps define and evaluate organizational success and supports the culture, goals, and objectives of the organization. "How" models trace directly to established values, guiding principles, and frameworks to ensure that the behaviors exhibited by teams reflect the values of the organization.

---

[6]Bouchard, Jim. *The Sensei Leader: Effective Leadership through Courage, Compassion and Wisdom*. Portland, Maine: San Chi Publishing, 2015.

An Operating System for Scalable Agility

At a recent appraisal of a very large-scale agile organization with more than three hundred Scrum teams, our appraisal team was looking for a way to gather more information about how certain agile ceremonies were being performed. Our solution? We executed an all-day Gemba Walk, whereby we strolled around two large towers watching teams perform standups, pair programming, planning poker, spring demos, and more. It quickly became obvious that, over time, teams had strayed dramatically from the true meaning of those ceremonies, some to the extent that they were no longer receiving value from them.

It was then that I decided a better model was needed, one that not only described the actions needed to adopt agile frameworks, but also described why and how to "be agile."

The design challenge was that all existing models from which to draw from attempted to depict "process" in two dimensions in a linear format. This was true of CMMI, PMBOK, ISO9001, ISO, and even, to some extent SAFe. This isn't how agile works.

Agile is object oriented, with guiderails that are instantiated by project teams who are free to improve them, and with services, ceremonies, and techniques being leveraged "as a service," which is why we never refer to scrum, xp, or other agile frameworks as a methodology or process – they are frameworks at best. Yet, people still try to draw flowcharts, swim lanes, or sequence diagrams to depict their agility.

AgileCxO's Agile Performance Holarchy (APH) is an organizational operating system that encapsulates all three layers, providing leaders with an integrated view of organizational agile performance.

APH provides agile leaders and teams with a model to build, evaluate, and sustain great agile behaviors and habits. It is not an agile maturity model or a process, but an operating system for sustainable agility. Figure 1-1 shows how APH defines performance circles and holons.

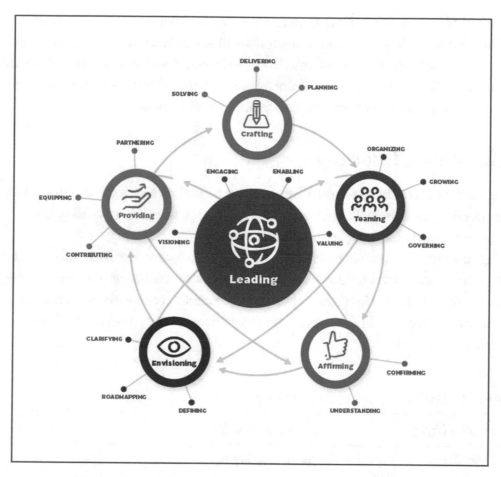

Figure 1-1. *The Agile Performance Holarchy*

Introduced in the 1967 book *The Ghost in the Machine* by Arthur Koestler, holons are described as self-reliant entities that "possess a degree of independence and can handle contingencies without asking higher authorities for instructions."[7]

Koestler further defines a holarchy as a "hierarchy of self-regulating holons that function first as autonomous wholes in supraordination to their parts, secondly as dependent parts in a subordination to controls on higher levels, and thirdly in coordination with their local environment."

A holarchy works well for describing and evaluating agile performance, where behaviors are self-organizing and empirical and the sequence of actions and outcomes is unpredictable, iterative, and recursive, rather than procedural.

---

[7]Koestler, Arthur. *The Ghost in the Machine*. Last Century Media, 1967.

The APH is composed of interdependent actions and outcomes that provide guidance for the behaviors, ceremonies, and techniques that might be performed to meet the outcomes by team members, functional groups, and leaders throughout the organization. Sequence, rigor, and intensity are determined by functional and project teams, not by management. There are several key APH components.

Performance Circles

Performance circles encapsulate a discrete set of behaviors with a set of actions and outcomes that are essential to successfully step through the process of adopting, transforming, and mastering large-scale agility.

Organizations wishing to benchmark performance against the APH may evaluate performance circles to determine how they are adopting, transforming, or mastering the behaviors of that circle. There are six performance circles, each with a specific objective for leadership, depicted in the classic user story format of role, mission, and business value (see Table 1-1).

Table 1-1. *Performance Circles and Objectives*

Performance Circle	Objective User Story
ENABLING, VALUING, Leading, VISIONING, ENGAGING	**As an** agile leader, **I want** to project agile values, provide the environment, and establish a vision **so that** my teams can be agile and successful in everything they do.

(continued)

Table 1-1. *(continued)*

Performance Circle	Objective User Story
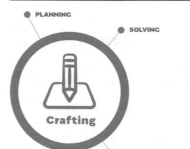	**As an** agile leader, **I want** agile team members engaged in the planning and building of high quality products **so that** we deliver the solution as expected.
	**As a** product owner, **I want** to establish a roadmap, release plan, and backlog **so that** the overall vision of the product or service can be realized.
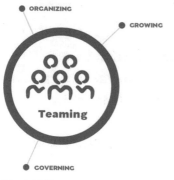	**As an** agile leader, **I want** teams and functional areas to learn and master self-organization and agile ceremonies and techniques **so that** the entire organization can benefit fully from agile adoption.

(continued)

Table 1-1. (*continued*)

Performance Circle	Objective User Story
Affirming (CONFIRMING, UNDERSTANDING)	**As an** agile leader, **I want** to confirm that teams are demonstrating agile values, methods, and techniques as expected **so that** I can understand what is working well and what needs improvement.
Providing (PARTNERING, CONTRIBUTING, EQUIPPING)	**As an** agile leader, **I want** to foster a continuous improvement environment and engage with agile partners **so that** agile teams can grow their capabilities.

Holons

Several holons are encapsulated within each performance circle, and they represent a set of actions and outcomes that can effectively stand alone but are also an integral part of a greater whole. All the actions and outcomes should be implemented in order to realize the value of each holon.

There are eighteen independent holons within the APH, as shown in Figure 1-2.

Leading	Crafting	Envisioning	Teaming	Affirming	Providing
Valuing	Planning	Road-mapping	Organizing	Confirming	Contributing
Enabling	Solving	Defining	Growing	Understanding	Partnering
Envisioning	Delivering	Clarifying	Governing		Equipping
Engaging					

Figure 1-2. *Holons within each performance circle define expected behaviors*

As an example, the engaging holon encourages the use of *gemba walks,* a process where leaders walk around to observe teams and "understand by seeing" in order to improve engagement and enable quality.

Objectives and Outcomes

Each holon describes objectives in a user story format that should be met in order to instantiate the value of the holon. An objective can be met by taking the defined actions in a manner and behavior that is consistent with agile values.

Holons contain a set of outcomes, like the performance circle they are surrounded by, which can be used to evaluate, improve, and sustain organizational agile performance within that context. The outcomes at the holon level are categorized into three levels, adopting, transforming, and mastering, and are used to help leaders evaluate and improve their organization's agile maturity.

For example, the objective and outcomes of the delivering holon, part of the crafting performance circle, are depicted as follows in Figure 1-3.

Adopting Level Outcomes	Transforming Level Outcomes	Mastering Level Outcomes
✳ Current state of organizational performance is defined.	✳ SWOT is complete and published.	✳ Organizational performance sprints are executed.
✳ Future state is identified and displayed.	✳ Backlog for future state exists in visual format.	✳ Progress is visually displayed using VIM.
	✳ Culture transformation release plan exists.	✳ Impediments to organizational performance are regularly identified and removed.

Figure 1-3. *Leaders can assess each holon's objectives and determine which outcomes have been met*

Actions

An action is the specific behavior that is applied to meet a holon's objective. All behaviors in the holon should be demonstrated in order to meet the intent of the objective, and each must always be aligned with agile values. The APH recommends agile ceremonies and techniques that, when executed successfully, will meet the intent of the actions. Not being a process, the APH does not require any ceremony or technique, although it does provide a list of potential options for those who wish to benefit from their guidance.

Ceremonies and Techniques

Each action provides a recommended set of ceremonies and techniques derived from agile and lean frameworks that can be adopted to demonstrate the desired behavior and meet the intent of the action.

The sixty-eight ceremonies and techniques described in the APH include all the typical visual information indicators, roles, expected behaviors, and actions, allowing leaders and all levels to effectively play their roles as servant leaders and recognize, evaluate, and enable improved organizational performance where needed.

Large-scale agility requires large-scale self-organization, but it isn't magic. Contrary to the claims of many agile-like practitioners that "agile doesn't use process," agile uses a lot of process; however, it may not be the kind you're used to. The freedom to successfully self-organize results in freedom through mastery.

Consider the martial artist, who goes through three distinct phases of maturity, starting with *shu*, progressing to *ha*, and final to *ri*—the master. At the *shu* stage, students learn their forms, practice their technique, and are committed to learning but have no expectations of high performance. At *ha,* students have increased confidence and are beginning to practice performance, often dangerously testing their boundaries only to learn they are not masters. Upon achieving *ri,* the student no longer thinks about what he or she learned during the prior two stages—it is built into their culture and they can practice their craft without a focus on *what*, only on *how.*

Self-organizing teams must also learn their craft, practice their forms, and progress through the stages of adopting, transforming, and mastering agility in order to be self-reliant.

Put in the Work and Reap the Rewards

According to VersionOne's "11th Annual State of Agile Report," 98 percent of respondents who believed they were agile reported success with agile projects.[8] That's a stunning statistic, but it isn't a coincidence. When agile works, the results are spectacular.

---

[8]VersionOne Inc. "11st Annual State of Agile Report." April 6, 2017. https://explore. versionone.com/state-of-agile/versionone-11th-annual-state-of-agile-report-2.

However, the same survey said that many organizations report a conflict between corporate policies and agile vales, that leadership lacked the skills to enable agile teams, and that more than half were still maturing years after adoption.

Successful agile organizations are not successful because they adopt popular ceremonies or frameworks. They are successful because they are committed to open, collaborative, and transparent servant leadership at all levels; and they have cultures where failure and risk are not punished, but celebrated as a way to learn and improve. Strong agile organizations are learning organizations that can demonstrate a mastery of self-organization.

For those companies, the behaviors they exhibit are the natural outcome of organizational culture change, and they produce better results when they align with the rules of nature, which consist of, among other things, iteration, continuous learning, incremental wins (and failures), transparency, and team collaboration. They succeed because they rely on trust, collaboration, and deep respect for team members; and they recognize that while teaming is highly valued, personal commitment to behavioral excellence is the prime directive. In other words, an agile culture aligns with the rules of nature, and successful agile teams are those that have mastered both self-organization and personal self-reliance.

Conversely, if an organization is autocratic, with a high degree of secrecy, distrust, and negativity; blames people for failures; and is generally low in trust, then they will struggle with agile adoption. Without an "operating system" upgrade, they can never realize the benefits of organizational agility. For those companies, adopting Scrum or Extreme Programming, both excellent frameworks, can be misleading. They *feel* agile, but, in practice, they are anything but. This will come back to bite them in the form of missed deadlines, high turnover, unhappy customers, low quality, and high cost. This eventually leads management to declare, "We tried agile, and it didn't work for us."

The Agile Performance Holarchy (APH) provides leaders and teams with an operating system that includes objectives, outcomes, and behavioral guiderails to succeed, along with an assessment method, training, and certifications to help chart a course to a high-performing agile future.

PART II

The Performance Circles

CHAPTER 2

Performance Circle: Leading

As an agile leader,

I will project agile values, provide the environment, and establish a vision,

So that my teams can be agile and successful in everything they do.

There is a reason the Leading Performance Circle comes first and is the largest circle in the Agile Performance Holarchy. Above all else, agile organizations must be led by agile leaders. Strong leadership is essential for successful self-organization – it's just not the kind of leadership you're used to.

Agile leaders must learn to empower their teams, and let them become the best they can be. They must abandon the fixed mindset, and embrace the growth mindset. Fixed leaders focus on risk, fear of failure, unchangeable constraints, and the consolidation of power. Growth leaders focus on lifelong learning for their teams and themselves, the success of others, organizational experimentation, failing fast, transparency, and customer collaboration. In other words, they themselves transform from "doing agile" to "being agile." Not so easy.

A successful agile leader masters the enablement of core values: responding to change, learning, empowerment, collaboration, transparency, failing fast, and more. Of all of the Performance Circles in the Agile Performance Holarchy, "Leading" is the most important (see Figure 2-1). Without leadership at all levels, frameworks such as Scrum and XP are just defined processes that force people to act as directed. With leadership and values, they become powerful, self-organizing, and enabling tools that can propel your organization to levels never before imagined.

© Jeff Dalton 2019

J. Dalton, *Great Big Agile*, https://doi.org/10.1007/978-1-4842-4206-3_2

Figure 2-1. *Leading*

Remember – don't do agile. Be agile.

The Leading performance circle describes actions, roles, and outcomes that address multiple levels of agile leadership. This circle provides guidance for agile leaders to define and deploy agile values, to provide an enabling infrastructure, develop an organizational vision for agility, and to fully engage as a leader that embraces agile values.

Agile leaders will benefit from learning to adopt, to embrace, and to deploy agile values and to cascade them throughout the leadership chain as they transition to a self-organizing leadership model.

By reviewing and learning about the elements of the Leading Performance Circle, successful agile leaders will learn to:

- Clearly demonstrate, articulate, and project agile values to peers, teams, and customers.

- Establish traceability from agile values to the frameworks, ceremonies, techniques, and behaviors that are adopted within their organization.

- Enable and encourage teams to own decisions about iterative scope, timing, tasking, and resource assignment.

- Engage with teams and customers to observe and evaluate agility.

- Enable continuous learning and iterative, incremental improvements across the organization.

Holon: Valuing

Valuing is a holon within the Leading performance circle. The Valuing holon describes a set of actions, outcomes, ceremonies and techniques that will help leaders define, deploy, project, and sustain agile values.

Objective

As an agile leader,

I want to define, deploy, project and sustain agile values,

So that my team understands the expectations for organizational agility.

Performance Level Outcomes

The Valuing holon has outcomes defined at each performance level. An organization can achieve performance outcomes by performing the actions and behaviors associated with the specific performance levels (see Table 2-1)

Table 2-1. *Valuing Performance Level Outcomes*

Adopting Level Outcomes	Transforming Level Outcomes	Mastering Level Outcomes
1. Agile values are selected and defined.	6. Essential stakeholders are engaged and demonstrate agile values.	9. Agile leaders at all levels are engaged in support of agile values.
2. Agile roles and accountabilities are defined.	7. Agile leaders are trained to live and project agile values.	10. Visual information management techniques are used to display project agile values.
3. Agile ceremonies and techniques are defined.	8. Agile values are prominently displayed throughout each facility.	11. Agile values are reevaluated, adjusted, and improved over time.
4. Agile teams are trained.		
5. Agile teams self-subscribe to established values.		

Action 1.0: Select and Define Agile Values

In order for organizations to become successful at embracing agile values, leadership begins by collaborating with teams to define the set of values the organization is best able to support given its mission, resources, and constraints. Clear values are a core necessity of any agile organization and manifest themselves in the behaviors demonstrated while using agile frameworks, ceremonies, and techniques. Roles and accountabilities of each individual should be defined and subscribed to at this time and mapped to the various techniques to be adopted.

Ceremonies/Techniques

- Open Space Technology

  Use the Open Spaces event for purpose-driven visioning and involve as many team members as possible in the selection and definition of agile values.

- Big Room Planning (BRP)

  While BRP is usually used for product and service planning, it can, and should, be used for organizational goal and values definition, where a cross-functional group of stakeholders work together to define and plan changes to the values, teams, and operations of the organization. BRP is best used when there is not significant ambiguity, and may be most useful after a successful Open Spaces event.

- Brainstorming

  Structured Brainstorming sessions can be used as a simplified alternative to Open Spaces events to collaborate with team members in the selection and definition of agile values.

- MindMapping

  MindMapping can be used as part of an Open Spaces event, or during Structured Brainstorming to help facilitate complex interdependencies.

- Value Tracing

  Value Tracing ensures that each value is traced directly to the set of frameworks, techniques, and behaviors that are adopted by teams.

Action 2.0: Communicate Agile Values

Agile values cannot survive in a vacuum, and solid communications is essential for their adoption. Once a manageable set has been selected and defined for each organization within a company, they will need to be socialized and communicated to all team members. Communications should include a clear description of its meaning and purpose within context of each organization, along with the expectations leadership has regarding the demonstration of values on projects and in other day-to-day behavior.

Ceremonies/Techniques

- Obeya Rooms

  Set up an Obeya Room to visually anchor and communicate agile values in a visible and transparent way. More than one Values Obeya Room can exist if multiple sites are being used, or if there are slight variations in values by location, function, or product line.

- Visual Information Management

  Visual information management techniques, which involve the use of outsized signs, boards, and digital medium through each facility, can be used as a constant reminder of the most important values.

- Gemba Walks

  Engage with team to reinforce leadership's understanding of, and passion for, agile values by conducting regular Gemba Walks. Leaders can see for themselves how well agile teams understand the selected values and can discuss their importance in real-time, providing coaching where needed. The regular presence of leaders in the area where work gets done will lead to a significant change in behavior.

Action 3.0: Deploy Agile Values

Agile values should be deployed to every corner of each organization within the company. This should include coaching and training for individuals on established roles and accountabilities related to each value, and for the selected agile techniques that are traced directly to each value. Structured coaching and mentoring for new agile practitioners by those who are more experienced should also be considered.

Ceremonies/Techniques

- Obeya Rooms

  Use an Agile Values Obeya Room to deploy agile values in a visible and transparent way. More than one Values Obeya Room can exist if multiple sites are used to do work.

- Gemba Walks

  Engage with teams to understand how well they understand the agile values. Ask questions and give feedback and coaching where needed to foster learning, but do not focus on compliance.

- Team Chartering/Team Agreements

  Agile values should be defined at the beginning of all Team Charters/Agreements, to encourage team members to self-subscribe to them, and understand how they relate to everyday work.

Action 4.0: Ensure Alignment of Agile Values

The methods, ceremonies, and techniques performed by agile teams are a manifestation of the organizational values. These behaviors should be visible to anyone observing teams in action. There is a strong relationship between the behaviors that agile teams exhibit and the values of the organization. If traceability between values and behaviors cannot be established, both should be reviewed to determine the impediment and actions needed to align them.

Ceremonies/Techniques

- Gemba Walks

  Leaders should see for themselves how aligned teams are to the established set of values. They can ask questions and give real-time feedback and coaching where needed to foster alignment.

- Enterprise Retrospectives

  Conduct values-based retrospectives in the Obeya Room, or with individual teams, to gather feedback on what is working well, what is not working well, and what could be improved related to agile values.

- MindMapping

  After observing team behaviors or conducting retrospectives, ensure behaviors align with organizational values in the values traceability MindMap.

- Enterprise Impediment Backlog

  Place impediments and improvements generated by values retrospectives on the Enterprise Impediment Backlog Board to ensure visibility and transparency.

Action 5.0: Maintain Agile Values

Agile values should be reviewed regularly to determine if they continue to serve the organization. Do not assume that selected values, and the behaviors that trace to them, will continue to be effective as the organization changes. Dedicate time to examine the behaviors, roles, and accountabilities, looking at methods, frameworks, and techniques in use by those teams. Opportunities for improvement should be identified and placed on the Enterprise Impediment Backlog.

Ceremonies/Techniques

- Gemba Walks

  Periodic observations, done on a regular schedule, will help encourage maintenance of values, and will allow leaders to see for themselves how aligned teams are to the established set. Questions can be posited to the teams, and real-time feedback and coaching can be provided.

- Lean Coffee

  Maintenance and strengthening of Agile values are best conducted informally, rather than "top down." Lean Coffee events are an excellent tool for sharing, receiving, and transmitting information.

- Enterprise Retrospectives

  Conduct values-based retrospectives directly with each team to gather feedback on what is working well, what is not working well, and what could be improved related to agile values.

- Enterprise Impediment Backlog

  Place impediments and improvements generated by retrospectives on the Enterprise Impediment Backlog to ensure visibility and transparency.

Holon: Engaging

Engaging is a holon within the Leading performance circle. The Engaging holon contains actions and ceremonies to support the development of a "servant leader" that engages, mentors, and participates with the organization's agile community.

Objective

As an agile "Servant Leader,"

I want to mentor and engage with agile teams,

To ensure agile values are being embraced, and to remove impediments to their adoption.

Performance Level Outcomes

The Engaging holon has outcomes defined at each performance level. An organization can achieve performance outcomes by performing the actions and behaviors associated with the specific performance levels (see Table 2-2).

Table 2-2. *Engaging Performance Level Outcomes*

Adopting Level Outcomes	Transforming Level Outcomes	Mastering Level Outcomes
1. Agile values are traced to frameworks, ceremonies, and techniques. 2. Constraints and impediments are identified and eliminated.	3. Agile teams use defined frameworks, ceremonies, and techniques. 4. Backlog that defines future state of performance is maintained.	5. Leaders at all levels of the business use defined agile frameworks, ceremonies, and techniques in their everyday work.

Action 1.0: Trace Agile Values to Frameworks, Ceremonies, and Techniques

The selected agile frameworks, ceremonies, and techniques will enable teams to demonstrate the behavior embodied by an organization's values. To ensure this is occurring, leadership should trace each value directly to each framework, ceremony, and technique being used by teams, and verify it through engagement and observation.

Ceremonies/Techniques

- Visual Information Management

  In the Obeya Room, common areas, or within team spaces, display agile values and their traceability to the frameworks, ceremonies, and techniques used by each team.

- Gemba Walks

  Observe their implementation of the ceremonies and techniques defined by each team. Provide feedback and coaching where needed.

- Lean Coffee

  Use periodic Lean Coffee events to share information between teams and management, and build trust across the organization.

Action 2.0: Engage with Agile Teams

Agile leaders should engage with teams on a regular basis to understand how values are being embraced throughout the organization. Engagement could take several forms, such as observing updates to information radiators, observing ceremonies and techniques in use, or reviewing the information generated through Retrospectives. This is especially critical in identifying and removing impediments that agile teams may be encountering. One of the best ways to empower self-organization and agile teams is for leadership to demonstrate their own commitment to engagement and agility.

Ceremonies/Techniques

- Visual Information Management

  Deploy a multilayered visual information management system at the project, group, and organizational levels including in Obeya Rooms, team spaces, conference rooms, and common areas.

- Gemba Walks

  Be present and engaged while observing team behaviors on a regular schedule.

- Retrospectives

  As a silent partner, attend selected retrospectives at multiple levels of the organizations to determine whether teams are focusing, in a structured way, on what is working well, what is not working well, and what could be improved.

- Scrum of Scrums

  Do not limit observations to the team level, but also observe rolled-up retrospectives, planning, and observations across teams using a structured Scrum of Scrums ceremony.

Action 3.0: Ensure Agile Leaders and Teams Are Embracing Agile Values

Agile values are not just for teams; leaders must also embrace them. Observing the behaviors of agile leaders, in the same way as teams are observed, provides valuable insight into the level of adoption and acceptance within the organization.

Ceremonies/Techniques

- Visual Information Management

  Display values in leadership areas, if they are separate from the team operations, including in all locations where leaders spend their time including executive conference rooms, dining areas, and the executive suite. Use simple information radiators that depict how well values are understood and lived by leaders in the projects and organization.

- Gemba Walks

  Observations should not be limited to teams, but should also include all levels of the organizational management.

- Retrospectives

  Conduct Leadership Retrospectives, using a similar format that is used by teams, to identify strengths, weaknesses, and improvement of management's adoption of agile and its values.

- Scrum of Scrums

  Observe your leaders at the individual team level, but also using the Scrum of Scrums construct to conduct Enterprise Retrospectives, planning, and reviews.

Action 4.0: Eliminate Impediments to Change

A critical role for all agile team members and especially agile leaders is to assist with the removal of obstacles that can prevent agile teams from meeting their commitments. Agile leaders need to ensure they are engaging with agile teams on a continual basis to help identify and remove constraints and obstacles that could occur.

Ceremonies/Techniques

- Gemba Walks

  Go and see agile teams in action. Observe their implementation of the ceremonies and techniques defined by the organization. Help them remove roadblocks and resolve constraints that are impeding their performance.

- Retrospectives

  Conduct Leadership Retrospectives with selected teams to understand how well your organization is supporting their use of agile frameworks and methods. Focus on what is working well, what is not working well, and what could be improved.

- Enterprise Impediment Backlog

  Record obstacles, constraints, and other impediments in the Enterprise Impediment Backlog. Use the backlog to visibly and transparently work with leaders and teams to remove impediments.

Holon: Visioning

Visioning is a holon within the Leading performance circle. The Visioning holon contains actions and ceremonies that help set and communicate a vision that is compatible with agile values and a healthy agile organization

Objective

As an agile leader,

I want to set and communicate a vision compatible with agile values,

So that we can develop a healthy agile organization.

Performance Level Outcomes

The Visioning holon has the following performance outcomes defined at each performance level. An organization can achieve performance outcomes by performing the actions and behaviors associated with the specific performance levels (see Table 2-3).

Table 2-3. *Visioning Performance Level Outcomes*

Adopting Level Outcomes	Transforming Level Outcomes	Mastering Level Outcomes
1. Current state of organizational performance is defined. 2. Future state is identified and displayed.	3. SWOT is complete and published. 4. Backlog for future state exists in visual format. 5. Culture transformation release plan exists.	6. Organizational performance sprints are executed. 7. Progress is visually displayed using VIM. 8. Impediments to organizational performance are regularly identified and removed.

Action 1.0: Understand Current Cultural State

Prior to beginning a transformation that leads to a healthy agile organization, a complete analysis of the current cultural state is required. An understanding of the strengths of its culture, as well as weaknesses that are impediments to success, needs to be identified in detail using the Agile Performance Holarchy as a baseline. In addition, opportunities and threats the organization will likely face during the cultural transition using a SWOT analysis should be identified.

Ceremonies/Techniques

- Strengths, Weaknesses, Opportunities, and Threats (SWOT)

  Use SWOT to openly and courageously identify the strengths of the current cultural state, weaknesses, and impediments to transformational change.

Action 2.0: Plan for Future Cultural State

Agile leaders should develop a plan to manage the transition from the current cultural state to the future state. The plan should be based on capabilities identified earlier and where the organizational culture is currently. The plan should identify the milestones, actions resources, and schedule needed for a successful transition.

Ceremonies/Techniques

- Class Responsibility Collaborator (CRC) Model

  Visualize the future cultural state through the use of CRC Cards. Use it as a thinking tool to define how the organization needs to change.

- SWOT

  Use the information in the SWOT to clearly identify the future state, and an initial road map to get there.

Action 3.0: Identify Impediments to Change

As with any attempt to culturally transform an organization, there will be barriers and obstacles encountered along the way. Left unchecked these impediments will negatively impact the organization's journey toward becoming a healthy agile organization. Leadership should take time to understand what these impediments are and how to best eliminate them as early as possible.

Ceremonies/Techniques

- SWOT

  Use SWOT to identify potential barriers and obstacles to organizational change.

- Enterprise Impediment Backlog

  Record the barrier and obstacles in a visual Enterprise Impediment Backlog. Use the backlog to visibly and transparently work with leaders to remove and mitigate the identified impediments.

Action 4.0: Sprint Toward the Future

Agile leaders should implement the future cultural state using an incremental and iterative approach that includes the use of backlogs, visual information management, sprints, sprint demos, and retrospectives. This allows agile leaders to balance several priorities, especially project work, while moving steadily toward the future state while demonstrating agile values.

Ceremonies/Techniques

- Enterprise Cascading Backlogs

  Use the outputs of SWOT or CRC Models to create a set of Enterprise Cascading Backlogs to plan out cultural changes.

- Enterprise Impediment Backlog

  Add actions to remove impediments identified in the Enterprise Impediment Backlog to the Enterprise Cascading Backlogs.

Holon: Enabling

Enabling is a holon within the Leading performance circle. The Enabling holon contains the actions and ceremonies required to design and deploy the set of "Agile Keys" that define the agile performance levels of Adopting, Transforming, and Mastering.

Objective

As an agile leader,

I want to design and deploy our set of Agile Keys,

So that our teams understand what is required to advance our performance level.

Performance Level Outcomes

The Enabling holon has the following performance outcomes defined at each performance level. An organization can achieve performance outcomes by performing the actions and behaviors associated with the specific performance levels (see Table 2-4)

Table 2-4. Enabling Performance Level Outcomes

Adopting Level Outcomes	Transforming Level Outcomes	Mastering Level Outcomes
1. Agile performance levels are identified for each holon. 2. Agile Keys for each level are used as is or customized for local context.	3. Agile teams are trained on Agile Keys. 4. Agile teams use Agile Keys to transform the way work is done.	5. Heartbeat Retrospectives are held. 6. Improvements from retrospectives are implemented.

Action 1.0: Select Agile Performance Level

Agile leadership determines which performance level (e.g., Adopting, Transforming, Mastering) it desires to achieve for each performance circle. The performance level will determine which Agile Keys are critical for the organization to embrace. There may be other factors that set the context, including business goals, the organization's agile experience, current capabilities, customer contracts, available resources, and more.

Ceremonies/Techniques

- Enterprise Cascading Backlogs

  Add to your Enterprise Cascading Backlogs all the actions needed to achieve a performance level. Include actions for all performance circles and holons in scope. Cascade actions down through impacted parts of the organization.

Action 2.0: Instantiate Agile Keys for Your Selected Level

Once leadership has selected the desired performance level, work should begin on the activities needed to build the supporting infrastructure and resources to allow the organization to effectively improve performance. Beyond infrastructure and resources, activities will focus on preparing the organization for the deployment of Agile Keys, such as organizational awareness, training, communications, and expectations communicated from leadership.

Ceremonies/Techniques

- Release Planning

  Use Release Planning to develop, size, and estimate overall performance improvement planning. Display results using visual information management techniques

- Sprint Planning

  Multiple sprint planning ceremonies should be used to identify, size, and prioritize cascading backlogs

- Enterprise Cascading Backlogs

  Use sprint planning to plan the first iteration of enterprise cascading backlog items. Focus on changes needed to instantiate the Agile Keys defined by the performance level and by your organization.

- Gemba Walks

  Observe how the first sprint is progressing across all cascading backlogs and teams. Ask questions and provide clarifications and coaching where needed.

Action 3.0: Deploy Agile Keys for Selected Performance Level

With assistance from leadership, the organization begins utilizing the infrastructure to support the implementation of Agile Keys. New roles and accountabilities become effective, expectations are communicated, training is provided, and project activities are reoriented toward an agile approach aligned with the desired performance level.

Ceremonies/Techniques

- Enterprise Cascading Backlogs

  Continue to use sprint planning to plan additional sprints of cascading backlog Items. Use visual information management to make progress visible and transparent.

- Gemba Walks

  Continue to go and see how sprints are progressing. Ask questions
  and provide clarifications and coaching where needed to maintain
  momentum.

Action 4.0: Sustain, Inspect, and Adapt Keys for Selected Performance Level

As the organization begins to adopt agile, progress and performance related
to demonstrating the Agile Keys will be continually reviewed to determine
effectiveness. Items that are working well should be reinforced and replicated
throughout the organization. Items that are not working quite as well should be
viewed as opportunities for learning, and improvements should be added to the
cascading backlog.

Ceremonies/Techniques

- Enterprise Cascading Backlogs

  Use your Enterprise Cascading Backlogs to plan improvements from
  Heartbeat Retrospectives, and remove impediments identified in the
  Enterprise Impediment Backlog.

- Enterprise Impediment Backlog

  Capture impediments identified in Gemba Walks and Heartbeat
  Retrospectives in the Enterprise Impediment Backlog. Make the
  Enterprise Impediment Backlog visible and accessible to all involved
  in the transformation.

- Heartbeat Retrospectives

  Do Heartbeat Retrospectives at a frequent enough pace to
  understand what is working well, what is not working well, and
  what should be improved. Add impediments to the Enterprise
  Impediment Backlog, and improvements to the Enterprise
  Cascading Backlogs.

CHAPTER 3

Performance Circle: Providing

As an agile leader,

I want to foster a continuous improvement environment, and engage with agile partners,

So that agile teams can grow their capabilities.

The Providing performance circle (Figure 3-1) describes the actions, roles, and outcomes related to providing an agile infrastructure. The organic nature of agile adoption has led some to believe that the leader has little responsibility to provide an infrastructure, but this has proven to be unrealistic at scale. The infrastructure might be different than what leaders have experienced thus far, but it is required nonetheless. Experienced leaders have learned that providing a solid infrastructure is essential to scaling agile across the enterprise.

Figure 3-1. *Performance Circle: Providing*

© Jeff Dalton 2019
J. Dalton, *Great Big Agile*, https://doi.org/10.1007/978-1-4842-4206-3_3

These infrastructure items include:

- Supplier contracts and Service Level Agreements (SLAs) with external suppliers that align with agile values, rather than traditional time and materials agreements.

- Continually improving and deploying best practices across the organization.

- Supporting agile Teams by providing automation tools and training.

Holon: Partnering

Partnering is a holon within the Providing performance circle. The Partnering holon contains the actions and ceremonies required to define relationships and agreements between teams and internal or external partners and suppliers.

Objective

As an agile leader,

I want to define relationships and agreements between teams and internal/ external partners and suppliers,

So that I can extend the capabilities of my agile teams.

Performance Level Outcomes

The Partnering holon has the following outcomes defined at each performance level. An organization can achieve performance outcomes by performing the actions and behaviors associated with the specific performance levels (see Table 3-1).

Table 3-1. *Partnering Performance Level Outcomes*

Adopting Level Outcomes	Transforming Level Outcomes	Mastering Level Outcomes
1. Multiple potential agile partners identified.	5. All key stakeholders are engaged with agile ceremonies.	8. Partner evaluation survey performed post agreement, and incrementally throughout the program.
2. Evaluation for the selection of agile partners was performed using criteria that maps to values.	6. Training provided for internal stakeholders on agreements and their alignment with agile values and methods.	9. Preferred partners are established using data about their alignment with agile values, and are known and understood to all teams.
3. Establish agreement with Partner that aligns with agile frameworks, methods, and techniques.	7. Verify that agreement aligns with agile values and methods.	
4. Develop partner communication plan.		10. Deploy agreements to all suppliers and partners that interact with delivery teams.

Action 1.0: Identify Internal and External Agile Partners

Determine which agile partners or suppliers are needed for a given project or organization. This may include internal groups or departments within an organization or external suppliers with whom an agreement is made. Other types of purchases include the ad hoc products or services. Project or organizational needs will be contained in a Product Road Map, but partner and supplier needs may be defined in Envisioning Sprints, Release Planning, or developing a Project Charter or Team Agreement.

Ceremonies/Techniques

- Envisioning Sprints

  An Envisioning Sprint is used to develop the Product Vision, which will identify products or services needing to be purchased from a partner or supplier.

- Release Planning

  Use Release Planning to plan for agile partner or supplier involvement during the upcoming release.

- Project Chartering/Team Agreements

  Use project chartering or team agreements to enable teams to define scope boundaries and mutual agreements between team and agile partner or suppliers.

Action 2.0: Assess Partner's Agile Capabilities

When the need for a partner has been identified, the organization should select multiple partners or suppliers that will satisfy the need. Assess each partner or supplier against the observable criteria in order to identify which will be selected. An Agile Partner Assessment ceremony, which includes the use of selected criteria and evaluation results, will assist in making a decision that is deliberate, defendable, and durable (the "Three D's" of agile decision making).

Ceremonies/Techniques

- Agile Partner Assessment

  Use the Agile Partner Assessment ceremony to evaluate multiple partners or suppliers in order to make the right selection.

Action 3.0: Develop Agile Partnering Agreement

Once a partner or supplier has been selected, an Agile Partnering Agreement will be created. Any agreement should align with the organization's agile values and framework, along with epics and stories that need to be satisfied, along with predefined acceptance criteria that must be met. Other considerations include how to address risk, customer participation, finances, scope, timing, and project transition.

Ceremonies/Techniques

- Agile Partnering Agreement

  Develop Agile Partnering Agreements to record terms to support an agile project.

Action 4.0: Engage with Partners Using Agile Partnering Agreement

Once an agreement or contract is in place, it should be incrementally monitored at sprint demos, and during sprint planning, until the work is complete. Identify all internal and external stakeholders that will be involved with the agreement. Develop a communication plan to assist with monitoring large projects that include rollup of Retrospective results and communications using a Scrum of Scrums construct. Plan for acceptance of any products or services that are being provided as part of the agreement using sprint demos.

Ceremonies/Techniques

- Acceptance Testing

  Perform acceptance testing using sprint demos or structured acceptance testing procdures.to ensure that the agile partner or supplier has delivered a product that meets the terms in their agreement or contract.

- Backlog Grooming

  Use backlog grooming to capture and adjust backlog prior to the next sprint.

- Release Planning

  Use release planning to plan for any agile partner or supplier involvement during the upcoming Release.

- Sprint Planning

  Include all agile partners or suppliers and their stories in sprint planning meetings to ensure they are engaged appropriately

- Stakeholder Identification and Management

  Ensure that agile partners or suppliers are included in the Stakeholder Engagement Plan, and monitor the plan using TeamScore to ensure engagement.

Holon: Contributing

Contributing is a holon within the Providing performance circle. The Contributing holon contains the actions and ceremonies required to identify, capture, and deploy lessons based on the empirical experience of agile teams.

Objective

As an agile leader,

I want to help teams identify, capture, and deploy lessons based on their experience,

So that we can improve our performance.

Performance Level Outcomes

The Contributing holon has the following outcomes defined at each performance level. An organization can achieve performance outcomes by performing the actions and behaviors associated with the specific performance levels (see Table 3-2).

Table 3-2. *Contributing Performance Level Outcomes*

Adopting Level Outcomes	Transforming Level Outcomes	Mastering Level Outcomes
1. Teams capture best practices for adoption.	5. Organizations capture enterprise-wide feedback.	9. Agile leaders support enterprise-wide ceremonies that include teams, partners, and suppliers.
2. Teams inspect and adapt performance.	6. Agile leaders are trained in how to capture, select, and deploy improvements.	10. Agile leaders collaborate with internal and external stakeholders on improvements.
3. Teams reflect on how to become more effective.	7. Best practices are leveraged across the organization.	
4. Improvements are adopted by projects.	8. Improvements are deployed across the organization.	

Action 1.0: Identify Best Practices

Agile teams plan to identify what is working well for the team. Team and enterprise best practices are captured regularly at all levels of the organization. Capturing best practices may be done by conducting project, enterprise, or functional area Retrospectives.

Ceremonies/Techniques

- Enterprise Retrospective

  Use the Enterprise Retrospective to capture experiences and
  organizational best practices in a Scrum of Scrums format.

- Retrospective

  Ensure agile teams conduct regular retrospectives to identify what
  went well and what should be improved in order to develop and
  capture best practices.

- Functional Retrospective

  Use the Functional Retrospective to capture experiences and best
  practice by functional group, including managers, engineers,
  developers, architects, and more.

Action 2.0: Share and Implement Best Practices

Agile leaders and teams review best practices captured during various types of
Retrospectives, and select what best practices should be adopted and shared with
the organization. Once selected, they are added to the improvement backlog for
implementation in sequence by priority. High-priority improvements are displayed
using the Best Practices Board.

Ceremonies/Techniques

- Best Practices Board

  Use a Best Practices Board to display and share best practices across
  teams.

- Improvement Backlog Grooming

  Use backlog grooming to prioritize best practices to be implemented.

Action 3.0: Identify Improvements

Agile teams should plan to identify practices that require improvements and prioritize what improvements can be made in a given sprint. The entire organization should capture improvement suggestions on a regular basis and share ideas across teams using a Scrum of Scrum formats. Capturing improvement suggestions may be done by conducting a Project Retrospective or Enterprise Retrospective Ceremony.

Ceremonies/Techniques

- Enterprise Retrospective

  Use the Enterprise Retrospective to identify improvements that can be implemented across teams.

- Retrospective

  Ensure agile teams conduct regular retrospectives to identify what did not go well and what action will be taken in order to continuously improve

Action 4.0: Share and Implement Improvements

Agile leaders and teams should review improvement suggestions captured during the various Retrospectives, then select which improvements should be adopted by the organization based on established criteria. Each improvement should be placed on the backlog and sequenced into an improvement sprint. Agile leaders should communicate improvements to the organization using the Best Practices Board.

Ceremonies/Techniques

- Best Practices Board

  Use a Best Practices Board to share the results of recent improvements across teams.

- Improvement Backlog Grooming

  Use backlog grooming to capture and track the implementation of suggested improvements.

Holon: Equipping

Equipping is a holon within the Providing performance circle. The Equipping holon contains the actions and ceremonies required to set up team space and equip the team with the tools to enable them to be an effective and successful self-organizing team.

Objective

As an agile leader,

I want to enable agile teams by equipping them with co-located space, tools, and training,

So that people have everything they need to succeed as a self-organizing team.

Performance Level Outcomes

The Equipping holon has the following outcomes defined at each performance level. An organization can achieve performance outcomes by performing the actions and behaviors associated with the specific performance levels (see Table 3-3).

Table 3-3. *Equipping Performance Levels*

Adopting Level Outcomes	Transforming Level Outcomes	Mastering Level Outcomes
1. Teams have a dedicated working space that aligns with localized agile values.	4. Team Space is set up in accordance with organization's agile values.	7. Agile leaders evaluate how team space and tools are working for team members.
2. Tools and automation are selected, identified, and available for team use.	5. Tools and automation meet project team needs.	8. Tools and automation are leveraged across all teams.
3. Training is conducted that meets team's needs.	6. Training is conducted on organizational values and tools for all team members.	9. The agile organization supports learning as a core capability.

Action 1.0: Acquire and Set Up Space for Teams

Agile leaders need to provide a working space for teams that is consistent with the core agile values of collaboration and transparency. This includes co-location, or effective tools that support virtual collaboration; collaborative work areas; work stations that support pair, mob, and team programming; preprinted rolling whiteboards; task boards with magnetic or paper cards; and outsized visual information indicators. Applying agile values to identify what the team needs may be done by conducting a Team Room Set-Up ceremony.

Ceremonies/Techniques

- Team Room Set-Up Meeting

  Use the Team Room Set-Up meeting to identify the work environment and finalize plans for implementation.

Action 2.0: Provide Tools for Teams to Use

Determine what tools are needed for the organization with a prioritization given to those that provide automation and increased efficiency. Stakeholders for tool decisions should include agile leaders, team members, support functions, and external tool providers.

Tools should be selected based on the organization needs, established values, and the Product Road Maps, which may include software for managing projects, stories, code, continuous build, quality, information radiators, and configuration management. Ceremonies where tool needs can be considered include Envisioning Sprints, Agile Partner Assessment, and brainstorming.

Ceremonies/Techniques

- Envisioning Sprints

  An Envisioning Sprint is used to develop Product Vision, which may include tools requirements or information radiators that are needed to meet short and long product needs.

- Agile Partner Assessment

  Use the agile partner assessment to evaluate potential tools in order to make a final selection.

- Brainstorming

  Use structured brainstorming to determine which tools or information radiators may be needed for the project and organization.

Action 3.0: Deliver Training and Mentoring

Agile leaders should ensure training is provided to the team based on values, as well as skills and tools. Refer to the Teaming performance circle for identifying training needs. Training should be planned, measured, and monitored to ensure effective delivery and knowledge transfer. Training may be delivered using different methods that include experiential training, instructor-led training, mentoring, coaching, or eLearning.

Ceremonies/Techniques

- Experiential Training

  Examine available experiential, hands-on training to determine what meets the training needs.

- Classroom Training

  Examine training needs to determine where classroom training is appropriate, and either groom instructors or identify an external training supplier.

- eLearning

  Examine training needs to determine where eLearning will be beneficial to the organization or project, implement a Learning Management System (LMS), and develop comprehensive eLearning content.

- Coaching and Mentoring

  Coaching and mentoring should be used as a sustainment tool, providing ongoing, iterative, and incremental reinforcement of initial training.

CHAPTER 4

Performance Circle: Envisioning

As a Product Owner,

I will establish a roadmap, release plan, and backlog,

So the overall vision of the product/ service can be realized.

The Envisioning performance circle describes actions and ceremonies that address the architecture required to define high-quality products and services (Figure 4-1). Behaviors demonstrated in the Envisioning performance circle include:

- Creating a product vision and road map to use as a guide for product development.

- Identifying and maintaining a product backlog to deliver the product vision.

- Clarifying customer needs into epics and user stories and ultimately system features to fulfill the product vision.

© Jeff Dalton 2019
J. Dalton, *Great Big Agile*, https://doi.org/10.1007/978-1-4842-4206-3_4

Figure 4-1. *Performance Circle: Envisioning*

Holon: Defining

Defining is a holon within the Envisioning performance circle. The Defining holon contains the actions and ceremonies required to build the product backlog that defines the product vision and road map.

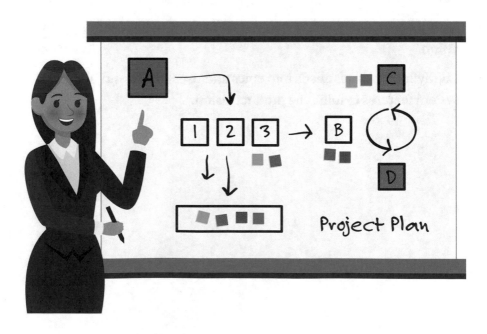

Objective

As a Product Owner,

I want to create a product backlog,

so that I have a list of prioritized features and functions which define the product vision.

Performance Level Outcomes

The Defining holon has the following outcomes defined at each performance level. An organization can achieve performance outcomes by performing the actions and behaviors associated with the specific performance levels (see Table 4-1).

Table 4-1. *Defining Performance Level Outcomes*

Adopting Level Outcomes	Transforming Level Outcomes	Mastering Level Outcomes
1. Backlog reflecting product vision with features and capabilities exists. 2. Product owners and agile team members are trained in the creation and management of the product backlog. 3. Cross-functional teams are effectively peer reviewing the backlog.	4. Product owner engages with agile team in all product ceremonies. 5. Prioritized and sized Product backlog exists. 6. Product Road Map exists with epics allocated over time. 7. Release plan is visually available and understood by all team members.	8. Multiple product backlogs are synchronized across agile teams. 9. Product backlogs are updated, refined, and kept current at all times. 10. Release plan is updated, refined, and kept current at all times. 11. Product definition ceremonies and techniques are improved and expanded over time.

Action 1.0: Allocate Road Map Work for Agile Teams

Based on the Product Road Map, the product owner will determine which elements of the Road Map will be allocated to which agile teams in order to produce the most positive outcome. Many companies maintain multilevel backlogs in support of synchronized agile teams in a Scrum of Scrums environment. Since this will involve the assignment of people and other resources, additional stakeholders within the organization may need to be consulted and integrated into the discussion of resource allocation and schedule

Ceremonies/Techniques

- Backlog Grooming

  Use backlog grooming to prioritize the initial set of items in the product backlog based on the Product Road Map, and determine which agile teams will be responsible for its implementation.

- Release Planning

  Engage in release planning to provide further detail based on the Product Road Map on when product features will be available.

Action 2.0: Develop Road Map Product Backlog

The product owner collaborates with the agile team to translate each desired feature, function, and product need defined in the road map into a set of functional and nonfunctional epics and stories. The information within the Product Road Map will evolve into a set of more detailed epics and stories within the product backlog.

Ceremonies/Techniques

- Backlog Grooming

  Use backlog grooming to collaborate within the teams, architects, and business analysts to transform functional and nonfunctional needs into an initial set of epics and user stories.

- Release Planning

  As further details are uncovered about the epics and stories in the product backlog, including dependencies and sizing, use release planning to refine the timing of when product functionality will be released.

- Three Diverse Humans

  Ensure that the backlog is peer reviewed early and often to ensure
  defects are driven out when they cause the least damage to the team
  and customer.

Action 3.0: Prioritize Road Map Product Backlog

After the product backlog is updated with the functional and nonfunctional product
epics and stories, the product owner collaborates with teams to prioritize them,
ensuring they align with the priority defined in the Product Road Map. During
this activity, the product owner and team will consider a number of factors that
include business value, clarity, risk, and dependencies, which help to establish
prioritization.

Ceremonies/Techniques

- Backlog Grooming

  Use backlog grooming to prioritize the epics and user stories in the
  product backlog.

- Release Planning

  Use release planning to reflect the priority in the product backlog
  regarding the timing of product features for release.

Holon: Road Mapping

Road Mapping is a holon within the Envisioning performance circle. The Road Mapping
holon contains the actions and ceremonies required to create the product vision, define
the product road map based on the vision, and identify the resources needed to make
the product a reality.

Objective

As a Product Owner,

I want to create a product vision and roadmap,

So that the team can utilize it as a guide for product development.

Performance Level Outcomes

The Road Mapping holon has the following outcomes defined at each performance level. An organization can achieve performance outcomes by performing the actions and behaviors associated with the specific performance levels (see Table 4-2).

Table 4-2. *Road Mapping Performance Level Outcomes*

Adopting Level Outcomes	Transforming Level Outcomes	Mastering Level Outcomes
1. Product vision reflects product needs and key functional/ nonfunctional attributes.	4. Cross-functional teams work to envision the overall product road map.	9. Product vision and road map updated over time and consistently kept up to date.
2. Product vision reflects product feasibility and key barriers.	5. Product vision reflects the target customers/ users.	10. Road mapping ceremonies and techniques are improved and expanded over time.
3. Road map aligns with product vision and describes product goals.	6. Product vision is compared against existing products for potential reusability.	
	7. Product vision reflects the product revenue model and value proposition.	
	8. Road map aligns with product vision.	

Action 1.0: Identify Current and Future Product Capabilities

Develop an understanding of the product's existing features and functions, and determine if its needs are being met. This information will describe the current product capabilities. Add future features and functions that will comprise the future state of the product. In the case of a new product, the focus should be on future capabilities the product needs to provide in its initial release.

Ceremonies/Techniques

- Big Room Planning

  Big Room Planning is best used when large, cross-functional teams need to collaborate to ensure complex solutions address the needs of the organization.

- Open Spaces

  Open Space Technologies can be used to explore vision and functionality if there is a significant number of unknown features that need to be extracted from the experiences of stakeholders and end users. It may make sense to conduct an Open Spaces event prior to Big Room Planning.

- Customer Interviews

  Use Customer Interviews to learn what new product features or changes to existing features that customers desire.

- Research Competitors

  Research Competitors to learn who the competitors are in your target market. Learn about product offerings from whom you are competing against.

- Product Comparisons

  Use Product Comparisons to understand how your offerings compare against other products from your competitors feature by feature.

- Market Research

  Perform Market Research to understand how to position your product in the market and differentiate it from the competition.

Action 2.0: Create Product Vision

Collaborate with stakeholders and other sources to create the product vision. The product vision should contain information defining the product across several dimensions. The product vision should be used as a tool to guide the product teams through the product development process.

Ceremonies/Techniques

- Envisioning Sprints

  Envisioning Sprints utilize agile methods to develop the Product Vision.

- Product Scenarios

  Use product scenarios to determine how an end user will interact with the product to achieve the end user's goal. The scenarios should focus on identifying what product features are required to provide benefits to the end user by using the product.

- Prototyping

  Use prototyping to build a less than fully functional version of the product in order to learn how the product will be perceived and used. Prototyping provides the agile team with invaluable information that can be used to refine the product's features.

- Kano Model

  The Kano Model provides an approach to determine what the most desirable features should be within a product to help differentiate it from competitors.

Action 3.0: Create Product Road Map

Once the product vision is created, define the approach and timing involved to make the product vision a reality using a Product Road Map. The product road map is especially useful for products where multiple versions are being planned. The road map brings together product release goals, release timing, and other key product characteristics that are affected by time. The road map is a living resource that will evolve over time along with the product itself.

Ceremonies/Techniques

- Envisioning Sprints

  Envisioning Sprints utilize agile methods to develop the Product Vision.

- Product Scenarios

  Use product scenarios to determine how an end user will interact with the product to achieve the end user's goal. The scenarios should focus on identifying what product features are required to provide a benefit to the end user by using the product.

- Prototyping

  Use prototyping to build a less than fully functional version of the product in order to learn how the product will be perceived and used. Prototyping provides the agile team with invaluable information that can be used to refine the product's features.

- Kano Model

  The Kano Model provides an approach to determine what the most desirable features should be within a product to help differentiate it from competitors.

Action 4.0: Define and Charter Agile Teams

Form the agile team(s) with the necessary knowledge and skills to implement the desired product features outlined in the product vision and road map. If the knowledge and skills needed are not available, the product owner will need to engage with other stakeholders (e.g., Senior Management, Human Resources, Third-Party Vendors) to recruit the needed technical expertise. Prospective team members without agile experience will also need training. Please see the Teaming performance circle for a definition of training outcomes.

Ceremonies/Techniques

- Team Agreements

  Team Agreements are used to define "rules of engagement" on how the team will interact with each other and those outside the team.

- Project Chartering

  Use Project Chartering to allow agile teams to self-organize around the key characteristics of their team. Let them create their "agile brand."

Holon: Clarifying

Clarifying is a holon within the Envisioning performance circle. The Clarifying holon contains the actions and ceremonies required to iteratively evolve the business needs into user stories, child stories, and tasks, and to better understand the customer's needs.

Objective

As a Product Owner,

I want to transform customer needs from the product backlog into epics and user stories,

So that agile teams can develop the product in an iterative and incremental fashion.

Performance Level Outcomes

The Clarifying holon has the following outcomes defined at each performance level. An organization can achieve performance outcomes by performing the actions and behaviors associated with the specific performance levels (see Table 4-3).

Table 4-3. *Clarifying Performance Level Outcomes*

Adopting Level Outcomes	Transforming Level Outcomes	Mastering Level Outcomes
1. Agile team members are trained in the development and analysis of user stories. 2. Product backlog representing Road Map consists of epics and stories.	3. Product owner engages with agile team during sprint planning, backlog grooming, and sprint demos. 4. Product backlog consists of epics and user stories that are prioritized, sized and traced to test cases and changes.	5. All product owners engage with respective agile teams across the organization. 6. Product backlog consists of epics, user stories, estimates, acceptance criteria, and the definition of done. 7. Clarifying ceremonies and techniques are improved and expanded over time.

Action 1.0: Evolve Business Needs into User and Child Stories

Functional and nonfunctional needs captured in the initial product backlog are reviewed by the product owner and agile team then transformed them into a set of user stories. As the user stories are created, acceptance criteria will be identified. Depending on the number of stories being created, it may be useful to group them into different themes to assist with organization.

Ceremonies/Techniques

- Backlog Grooming

    Use backlog grooming to collaborate within the agile team to prioritize functional and nonfunctional needs into epics and user stories.

Action 2.0: Refine the Product Backlog

The user stories in the product backlog are reviewed on a regular basis by the product owner and the agile teams. The goal is to ensure the stories in the product backlog meet the team standards related to the definition of ready before the story can be considered for inclusion within an upcoming sprint. An important aspect to definition of ready includes applying established criteria to each story.

Ceremonies/Techniques

- Backlog Grooming

  Use backlog grooming to provide more detail to the epics and user stories reflecting new dependencies and recent priorities. The epics and stories are refined until the definition of ready is met.

Action 3.0: Size the Product Backlog Items

User stories, which have undergone refinement by the product owner and agile team, are sized for inclusion in an upcoming sprint. The developers on the team will use various techniques (e.g., T-shirt Sizing, Planning Poker) to estimate each story. In some instances, the sizing exercise may point to the need for additional product backlog refinement.

Ceremonies/Techniques

- Backlog Grooming

  Use backlog grooming to prioritize each user story once a sufficient level of detail has been reached.

- Relative Estimation

  Use relative estimation to size or group user stories, tasks, and subtasks on a comparison basis using complexity as a driving factor.

- Team Estimation Game

  Team estimation is used by the agile team to collectively estimate items in the product backlog using relative estimation.

- Release Planning

  As user stories are sized, use release planning to refine the timing of when product features are released.

CHAPTER 5

Performance Circle: Crafting

As an agile leader,

I want agile team members engaged in the planning and building of high quality products,

So that we deliver the solution as expected.

The Crafting performance circle describes objectives, actions, and ceremonies that address the capability lift and craftsmanship required to consistently deliver high-quality products and services (Figure 5-1).

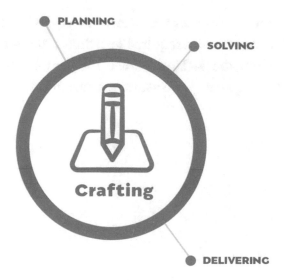

Figure 5-1. *Performance Circle: Crafting*

© Jeff Dalton 2019
J. Dalton, *Great Big Agile*, https://doi.org/10.1007/978-1-4842-4206-3_5

Agile leaders need to instill a culture of craftsmanship in their own organization as well as other organizations within the product or service value stream. Customers, procurement, and sales all have a role to play, and for technologists to be successful, leaders from those organizations need to demonstrate craftsmanship as well.

Some components of Craftsmanship include:

- Integrated coding-design-testing techniques such as test-driven development (TDD) and business-driven development (BDD).

- Effective strategies for managing technical debt and refactoring.

- Eliciting and recognizing high-quality requirements, epics, and stories.

- Engagement of the business and end users for product ownership and relevant ceremonies.

- Implementation of an effective tool chain with sufficient automation across the entire product or service development life cycle.

Holon: Planning

Planning is a holon within the Crafting performance circle. The Planning holon contains the actions and ceremonies required to estimate and plan for the upcoming sprint or iteration, grooming the backlog by the team, demonstrating successes, and inspecting and adapting team performance as part of continuous learning and improvement.

Objective

As an agile leader,

I want agile team members to estimate and plan for the upcoming sprint and groom the backlog mid-sprint,

So that we meet the sprint forecast is met as planned.

Performance Level Outcomes

The Planning holon has the following outcomes defined at each performance level. An organization can achieve performance outcomes by performing the actions and behaviors associated with the specific performance levels (see Table 5-1).

Table 5-1. *Planning Performance Level Outcomes*

Adopting Level Outcomes	Transforming Level Outcomes	Mastering Level Outcomes
1. Projects demonstrate the use of established agile planning ceremonies and techniques. 2. Agile values are demonstrated during planning. 3. Project team members are trained in the agile planning ceremonies and techniques.	4. Essential planning stakeholders engage with projects while demonstrating agile values. 5. Agile leaders are trained in agile planning ceremonies and techniques, and use them for their own work. 6. All projects and functional groups use agile planning ceremonies and techniques.	7. Projects select planning ceremonies and techniques based on project needs and objectives. 8. Agile leaders engage with projects using agile values. 9. Planning ceremonies and techniques are improved and expanded over time.

Action 1.0: Enable Team Commitment

A culture of agile leadership demonstrates core agile values top-down and bottom-up at all times to enable self-organization of all project teams. Project chartering and Team Agreements define the agile brand of each team.

Ceremonies/Techniques

- Project Chartering/Team Agreement

  Use project chartering/team agreements to enable agile teams to self-organize around the key characteristics of their team's values, goals, and objectives. Each team creates their personal "agile brand," which can include behaviors, operations, and a unique team name.

- Self-Subscription

  Foster a culture of team commitment and self-organization by
  ensuring all agile team members are empowered to self-subscribe
  (pull) work from a backlog based on their availability, expertise, and
  workload. Self-subscription is a core behavior of lean thinking, and is
  a powerful tool for promoting agility across teams.

Action 2.0: Create and Agree on a Definition of Done

Backlog grooming, mid-sprint can be used to ensure that a surplus of user stories is
always available for the next iteration or sprint. A definition of done is clearly defined
for each story, with common criteria captured in team agreements as part of the teams'
agile brand.

Ceremonies/Techniques

- Project Chartering/Team Agreements

  Use project chartering/team agreement to self-organize around the
  key characteristics of their team, and the definition of done for epics,
  stories, code, tests, and more. Let them create their "agile brand."

- Team Agreements

  Use team agreements to capture common definitions of done.

- Definition of Done

  Use definition of done to capture, in unambiguous language, how
  the team knows a user story is complete and ready to present to the
  product owner or other stakeholders in a sprint demo.

- Backlog Grooming

  Use backlog grooming to generate and capture the forecast for
  subsequent sprints, and define the definitions of done for individual
  user stories that are being considered.

Action 3.0: Select Work to Complete for Each Sprint

Self-subscription enables the agile team members who are doing the work to pull from a backlog(s) of prioritized user stories. A Definition of Ready is clearly defined and verified for each story on the backlog to ensure they are ready to be selected.

Ceremonies/Techniques

- Incremental Development

  Use an incremental approach to break development into small, consistent, manageable, and predicable pieces.

- Definition of Ready

  Use a common definition of ready to increase the likelihood that the team is working with high-quality stories, and that the implementation of a user story in each increment will be successful. Applying screening criteria such as INVEST to user stories is an example of definition of ready.

- Self-Subscription

  Foster a culture of ownership by empowering agile teams to employ self-subscription while they pull their own work from the backlog. Self-subscription support ownership and commitment with self-organizing teams. Employ self-subscription in all sprint planning and grooming meetings.

Action 4.0: Estimate the Work to Complete in the Sprint

Sprint planning meetings are used to size user stories relative to one another using techniques such as Planning Poker, T-Shirt Sizing, or the Team Estimating Game. As part of planning the upcoming sprint or iteration, team members break the selected user stories into tasks, and then estimate each task in hours to complete. Tasks include activities beyond coding proven to support craftsmanship such as design, unit testing, prototyping, and validation/verification.

Ceremonies/Techniques

- Relative Estimation

  Use relative estimation to size epics and user stories as larger or smaller than a known, agreed-upon reference. Limit choices and ranges in the Team Agreement to increase estimation consistency, and reduce the time needed to create estimates.

- Team Estimation Game (Planning Poker)

  Use the Team Estimation Game or Planning Poker, to size user stories as part of sprint planning. Encourage "relatively right" versus "accurately wrong" estimates using Planning Poker based on a limited-range Fibonacci sequence.

- Backlog Grooming

  Use backlog grooming to prioritize stories for future sprints.

- Sprint Planning

  Include the sprint planning meetings to engage agile team members and the product owner in the estimation and planning process. Team members should break down user stories into the tasks (in hours) needed to complete the story and meet the predefined definition of done.

Holon: Solving

Solving is a holon within the Crafting performance circle. The Solving holon contains the actions and ceremonies needed to create and sustain high-quality products and services from the viewpoint of the customer. Solving is a structured and disciplined approach to the design and development of products and services. Craftsmanship starts here.

Objective

As an agile leader,

I want to help agile team members meet their sprint forecast,

So that we develop a high-quality solution using an iterative and incremental approach.

Performance Level Outcomes

The Solving holon has the following outcomes defined at each performance level. An organization can achieve performance outcomes by performing the actions and behaviors associated with the specific performance levels (see Table 5-2).

Table 5-2. *Defining Performance Level Outcomes*

Adopting Level Outcomes	Transforming Level Outcomes	Mastering Level Outcomes
1. Teams use established product development ceremonies and techniques.	4. Essential product development stakeholders demonstrate agile values.	7. Teams proactively select product development ceremonies and techniques based on project needs, objectives, and constraints.
2. Agile values are demonstrated during product development.	5. Agile leaders are trained in how to recognize established product development ceremonies and techniques.	8. Agile leaders engage with teams using agile values.
3. Team members are trained in the established product development ceremonies and techniques.	6. All teams in the organization select product development ceremonies and techniques from a common set.	9. Product development ceremonies and techniques are improved and expanded over time.

Action 1.0: Burn Down User Stories

Project teams demonstrate self-organization and commitment by completing the implementation of user story tasks for the current sprint or iteration without oversight from a project manager. Disciplined methods are used to complete work, with a focus on quality, and visual information management systems create transparency for all team members and extended stakeholders.

Ceremonies/Techniques

- Burn Down Chart

  Display daily progress and work that has been completed during each sprint using a burn down chart. Any stakeholder can easily determine if the sprint forecast will be met. Action can be taken early to reprioritize stories and tasks.

- Scrum Wall

  Use a scrum wall to show the progression of user stories through the workflow states defined by the team in the team agreement. The scrum wall and burn down charts, used together, create transparency for all stakcholders.

- Kanban Board

  For teams that use Kanban to manage work, use a Kanban Board for visual information management.

- Velocity

  Velocity, in story points, represents the capacity of a team to deliver value during a sprint. Once established, it creates predictability for each sprint and the overall release plan, given a relatively consistent team.

- Pair Programming

  Use pair programming for low-defect product development. Although counterintuitive, it is consistently more efficient than working individually.

- Mob Programming

  Mob programming adds the whole team, not just the developers, to the development effort. Adding different perspectives early reduces all sources of defects.

- Test-Driven Development

  Use test-driven development to create tests first, and then write code that fails or passes the tests. Working this way increases efficiency by getting both the tests and the code right early in the development cycle.

- Unit Testing

  Do unit testing finds and eliminate defects early in the development cycle. Automated unit testing is common with agile teams, and it is encouraged for 100 percent of all code.

Action 2.0: Review Activities and Impediments

The team has discussed progress and transparently identifies impediments as a group. The daily standups have a short, focused script, defined in the team agreement, are time boxed, and are facilitated by a scrum master or equivalent. Impediments are recorded in an impediment backlog so they can be addressed outside of the daily stand-up.

Ceremonies/Techniques

- Daily Stand-Up/Daily Scrum

  The Daily Stand-Up, also known as the Daily Scrum, Huddle, or Daily Meeting, significantly increases transparency and collaboration for the team. The better and more open the daily stand-up is, the higher the likelihood of rapidly solving problems to ensure meeting sprint commitments.

- Impediment Backlog

  Use an Impediment Backlog to quickly record impediments that cannot be addressed during the daily stand-up. Use Visual Information Management for the Impediment backlog to increase visibility and transparency.

Action 3.0: Remove Impediments

Impediments in the impediment backlog are eliminated, if possible, by the Scrum Master or agile leader. Impediments that cannot be eliminated are used to identify future improvements, or are escalated to the agile leadership so they can be resolved for the benefit of the entire organization.

Ceremonies/Techniques

- Impediment Backlog

  Continuously improve quality and performance by eliminating impediments recorded in the Impediment Backlog. Instill the value of "Inspect and Adapt."

Action 4.0: Review Completed Work

The customer or end user of the product or service reviews and accepts or rejects what was completed by the team during the current sprint or iteration. The customer or end user accepts the work, identifies changes to be made, or identifies new needs or stories for a future sprint or iteration. Prioritization of changes or new stories is defined and agreed upon.

Ceremonies/Techniques

- Sprint Demo

  Use the Sprint Demo, also known as a Sprint Review, or Show and Tell, to capture immediate feedback from the customer or business owner of the product being demonstrated. Capture both defects and change requests at this time to efficiently manage changes and improvements.

Action 5.0: Identify Improvements

The project team conducts a retrospective after each sprint to identify improvements and learning opportunities. The retrospective is facilitated by a scrum master, or equivalent, and appropriate learning information is shared beyond the boundaries of the project team so the entire organization benefits.

Ceremonies/Techniques

- Sprint Retrospective

  Ensure the team conducts Sprint Retrospectives to identify what went well (continue doing), what did not go well (stop doing), and what should be improved (learning) for the next sprint. Share appropriate learning with all teams doing similar work.

- Milestone Retrospective

  Do Milestone Retrospectives to collaborate with additional stakeholders outside the localized agile team.

Holon: Delivering

Delivering is a holon within the Crafting performance circle. The Delivering holon contains the actions and ceremonies needed to plan product or service releases at a higher level than individual sprints or iterations. Delivering contains planning how product assembly and testing are done at the sprint or iteration level, and at the release level, as well as how and when the assembled and tested product is made available to the customer or end user.

Objective

As an agile leader,

I want team members to integrate and test the solution,

So that it meets the needs of the customer and end-user.

Performance Level Outcomes:

The Delivering holon has the following performance outcomes defined at each performance level. An organization can achieve performance outcomes by performing the actions and behaviors associated with the specific performance levels (see Table 5-3)

Table 5-3. *Delivering Performance Level Outcomes*

Adopting Level Outcomes	Transforming Level Outcomes	Mastering Level Outcomes
1. Projects use defined delivery ceremonies and techniques. 2. Agile values are demonstrated during delivery. 3. Project team members are trained in the defined delivery ceremonies and techniques.	4. Essential delivery stakeholders engage with projects using agile values. 5. Agile leaders are trained in the delivery ceremonies and techniques. 6. All projects use defined delivery ceremonies and techniques.	7. Projects proactively select organizational delivery ceremonies and techniques based on project needs, objectives, and constraints. 8. Agile leaders engage with projects using agile values. 9. Delivery ceremonies and techniques are improved and expanded over time.

Action 1.0: Plan each Delivery

The product owner, or their equivalent, creates a release plan that connects the completion of the stories in each sprint or iteration to individual releases. The release plan is at a level higher than the individual sprints or iterations, and is continuously updated and communicated to the team as part of backlog grooming.

Ceremonies/Techniques

- Release Planning

  Identify the high-level release schedule and the goal for each release by doing release planning. Work to deliver the highest value (from the perspective of the end user) user stories early in the development.

- Backlog Grooming

  Use backlog grooming to target user stories for planned releases.

Action 2.0: Assemble Product or Service Component for the Sprint

The assembly of the product or service components are accomplished using the methods and tools defined as part of release planning. Automated builds and continuous integration are used to improve efficiency, quality, and the craftsmanship of the end product or service.

Ceremonies/Techniques

- Automated Build

  Use Automated Builds to build code modules, and run automated unit tests each time code is checked-in. Bias the process towards rapidly finding and fixing defects early (fail fast).

- Continuous Integration

  Use Continuous Integration to build the product at the component level, and run automated integration tests each time the product is built. Bias the process towards rapidly finding and fixing defects at the interface level.

Action 3.0: Test Assembled Product or Service

The assembled product or service is tested to make sure performance matches the expectations and commitments made during the sprint or iteration. Detailed information is captured for defects, enabling root cause analysis, and resolution occurs within the sprint or iteration, or de-prioritized and added to the backlog. The team analyzes defects or bugs, and uses the information gathered for future retrospectives to drive continuous learning and improvement.

Ceremonies/Techniques

- Acceptance Testing

  Conduct Acceptance Testing to ensure that product works correctly
  for the end user. If possible, the customer or end-user should perform
  testing in the presence of the team via the Sprint Demo.

- Usability Testing

  Leverage Usability Testing to ensure that the end-user will have a
  positive impression of the user experience.

Action 4.0: Deliver the Assembled Product or Service

The product or service is delivered to the customer or end-user as defined in the release
plan. Changes or defects identified after delivery are placed on the backlog, reviewed
with the customer or end-user, prioritized, and sequenced into future sprints or
iterations.

Ceremonies/Techniques

- Continuous Deployment

  Using automation, promote the assembled and tested product to the
  production environment at the end of each sprint to receive rapid
  feedback from the user community.

- Frequent Releases

  When automated build is not possible, promote the assembled and
  tested product in the production environment at a rapid cadence to
  receive frequent feedback from the user community.

CHAPTER 6

Performance Circle: Affirming

As an agile leader,

I want to confirm that teams are demonstrating agile values, methods and techniques as expected,

So that I can understand what is working well and what needs improvement.

The Affirming performance circle describes actions, ceremonies, and roles that address the observation of team performance (Figure 6-1). The Affirming performance circle is about confirming that all team members, including management, are walking the walk," and the products that are built are meeting the needs of the business customers.

Figure 6-1. *Performance Circle: Affirming*

© Jeff Dalton 2019
J. Dalton, *Great Big Agile*, https://doi.org/10.1007/978-1-4842-4206-3_6

Agile leaders need to demonstrate techniques for useful, yet lightweight, evaluation of team behavior. Some of these include:

- Perform "Gemba Walks" using passive observation techniques.

- Conduct retrospectives with cross-functional teams to help team members self-realize the importance of agile values and have sufficient knowledge of the expected behaviors in a healthy agile organization.

- Gather feedback and information from metrics and surveys and use it to improve performance.

Holon: Understanding

Understanding is a holon within the Affirming performance circle. The Understanding holon contains the actions and ceremonies required to collect and analyze metrics in order to understand team and organizational performance and quality. This understanding leads to corresponding actions needed to improve target areas.

Objective

As an agile leader,

I want to know if we are receiving the benefits of agile adoption,

So that the business can understand its performance and find ways to improve.

Performance Level Outcomes

The Understanding holon has the following outcomes defined at each performance level. An organization can achieve performance outcomes by performing the actions and behaviors associated with the specific performance levels (see Table 6-1).

Table 6-1. *Understanding Performance Level Outcomes*

Adopting Level Outcomes	Transforming Level Outcomes	Mastering Level Outcomes
1. Agile teams are collecting basic velocity metrics to understand their performance.	6. Teams adopt a shared set of organizational metrics that are used to understand their collective performance.	9. Performance metrics from teams and functional areas are aggregated and trended to understand organizational performance.
2. Agile teams are collecting basic metrics to understand the quality of the products they are developing.	7. Teams adopt a shared set of organizational metrics that are used to understand the quality of the products they are developing.	10. Product quality metrics from agile teams are aggregated and trended to understand organizational product quality.
3. Metrics are visibly displayed.	8. Metrics are utilized and reviewed during agile ceremonies, for example, sprint planning and retrospectives.	11. Agile teams are using metrics to improve performance and quality.
4. Metrics are reviewed regularly by the team.		12. The organization is using metrics to improve performance and quality.
5. Teams are meeting to discuss outcomes and solve problems.		

Action 1.0: Identify Metrics to Understand Project, Product, Team, and Process Performance

Determine what metrics will be used to understand performance. Agile CxOs, leaders, and scrum masters, product owners, and teams should collaborate to identify and prioritize the metrics that will provide the most value in determining project, product, team, and process performance. The Goal, Question, Indicator, Metric (GQM) technique may be used to assist with identifying metrics to align with business goals. Other techniques that may assist with metrics selection are visual information management and retrospectives.

Ceremonies/Techniques

- Goal, Question, Metric (GQM)

  Use GQM to identify and define organizational goals, information needs, measurement objectives, and metrics. Ensure there is traceability from goals to metrics so that progress toward goal achievement can be understood.

- Visual Information Management

  Use visual information management to make the measurement program visible and transparent.

- Retrospectives

  Use retrospectives to gather improvement information for the measurement program. Record relevant metrics and outcomes.

- Lean Coffee

  Conduct Lean Coffee events as a way for the team to informally communicate, review performance, and solve problems.

Action 2.0: Collect and Report Metrics Data

Metrics data should be captured and reported based on goals identified by the organization at various levels. Responsibility for collecting metrics and reporting should be assigned to specific roles based on point of capture so there is no confusion or overlap. Metrics data should be reported via information radiators in accordance with the visual information management strategy.

Ceremonies/Techniques

- Visual Information Management

  Use visual information management to make metrics data and progress toward goal achievement visible and transparent.

- Retrospectives

  Use Team and Enterprise Retrospectives to understand what metrics are providing useful data, what metrics are not providing useful data, and to identify improvements or new metrics to create.

- Scrum of Scrums

  Individual and aggregate metrics should be reviewed and discussed in a cross-functional team construct, such as a Scrum of Scrums event, across teams and functional groups.

Action 3.0: Analyze and Trend Metrics Data

Once metrics are collected and reported, they will need to be analyzed. Analysis should include a review of metrics for trends, or comparing results against targets to assist with interpreting the data. This information should be used by leaders to understand team performance. Ceremonies that may be used to assist with analysis include evaluation, retrospectives, and reviews. The visual information management strategies will identify which information radiators provide the best medium trend analysis.

Ceremonies/Techniques

- Evaluation

  Involve key stakeholders in the evaluation of data to understand what each metric actually means in the context of the strategic goals and measurement program. Identifying and understanding trends is a key part of evaluation.

- Visual Information Management

  Use visual information management to trend metrics data and trend progress toward goal achievement. Information radiators should show a history for metrics that collected over time.

- Retrospectives

  Use retrospectives to understand positive trends, trends that are not going as expected, and to identify improvements or changes to address trends that are not going as expected.

- Review

  Share the trends and interpreted data during a Review with each team and each level of the organization. Make the Review of data a key ceremony in your suite of Agile Techniques.

Action 4.0: Identify Actions to Improve Performance

Once the results of metrics are understood, identify what actions are needed. Analysis of metrics could lead to confirming if the metric is providing value, whether the metric needs to be modified to improve value, or action needed to address a finding. Taking action is important to support continuously improving performance. Identified action items should be monitored and tracked to closure. Ceremonies where actions may be identified include evaluation, information radiators, and retrospectives. The visual information management technique may identify which information radiators will track improvements.

Ceremonies/Techniques

- Evaluation

  As part of Involving key stakeholders in the evaluation of data, identify what actions, if any, are needed to address data trends that are not going as expected.

- Visual Information Management

  Add actions identified during the evaluation of the metrics to backlogs or other information radiators so they are visible and transparent to all involved.

- Retrospectives

  Use retrospectives to gather improvement information for the measurement program. Add them to the visual information management systems being used.

- Review

  Review actions with owners and stakeholders to make sure actions are being completed, and all stakeholders are aware of progress.

Holon: Confirming

Confirming is a holon within the Affirming performance circle. The Confirming holon contains the actions and ceremonies required to understand how agile has been adopted by the team. This information can then be used to improve agile team performance.

Objective

As an agile leader,

I want to evaluate how well team members adhere to agile values, frameworks, and techniques,

So that I can understand where there are opportunities to improve team performance.

Performance Level Outcomes

The Confirming holon has the following outcomes defined at each performance level. An organization can achieve performance outcomes by performing the actions and behaviors associated with the specific performance levels (see Table 6-2).

Table 6-2. *Confirming Performance Level Outcomes*

Adopting Level Outcomes	Transforming Level Outcomes	Mastering Level Outcomes
1. Agile coach is assigned to each team and functional area.	4. Leaders regularly observe teams and functional areas in person.	6. Coaches identify best practices and team improvements that can be shared across teams and functional areas.
2. Coaches are regularly observing and evaluating teams and functional areas.	5. Teams and functional areas identify and implement performance improvements based on the feedback they receive from coaches and leaders.	7. Enterprise Retrospectives utilize feedback from coaches and leaders to improve performance across teams and functional areas.
3. Coaches are regularly providing feedback to teams, functional areas, and leaders.		8. Leaders use data to confirm that teams and functional areas are adopting values and techniques.

Action 1.0: Observe Adoption of Agile Behaviors

In order to understand how well agile is working in your organization, it is important to observe behaviors and outcomes. Observation should be done regularly and not be disruptive to the ceremony or event in progress. Some techniques that may be helpful are the Gemba Walk and Evaluation.

Ceremonies/Techniques

- Gemba Walk

  Passively observe teams in action to understand how well they are living their agile brand.

- Evaluation

  Meet with teams and functional areas, ask questions, and share your observations with them, and coach them where appropriate. Share their strengths and how they can strengthen areas of weakness.

Action 2.0: Gather Information from Agile Teams about Their Adoption of Agile Behaviors

Observations and team input are gathered for understanding the adoption of agile values, methods, and techniques. Input may come from any ceremony or event where adoption is demonstrated. The techniques that help understand adoption behavior include the Gemba Walk, Evaluation, Review, and Kamishibai Board.

Ceremonies/Techniques

- Gemba Walk

  Have each team send an emissary to observe how other teams have adopted agile, and to gather feedback and improvement ideas across teams.

- Evaluation

  Identify key stakeholders to do cross-evaluations of other teams. Consolidate the information at the organization level.

- Review

  Share the all the information gathered as part of Gemba Walks, evaluations, and Kamishibai checks with the stakeholders.

- Kamishibai Board

  Use a Kamishibai Board to plan a dynamic set of agile checks, and to involve the immediate team members and two or more levels above them in the leadership chain.

Action 3.0: Provide Improvement Feedback to Agile Teams

Agile leaders and agile coaches provide feedback to teams and functional areas. It is important to provide the feedback information about behaviors early and often. Techniques that will provide feedback include the Gemba Walk, Evaluation, Review, and Kamishibai Board.

Ceremonies/Techniques

- Gemba Walk

  Results of observations made during Gemba Walks should be shared with teams and functional areas early and often.

- Evaluation

  Meet with teams and functional areas often to review and analyze the gathered observations to determine actions that need to be taken to improve performance.

- Review

  Review the actions from the evaluations and encourage team members to self-subscribe to actions for improvements.

- Kamishibai Board

  Add changes that were made to the cards pulled for the Kamishibai Board.

Action 4.0: Use Improvement Feedback to Improve Agile Team Performance

Agile teams and functional areas should use feedback generated from observations to improve team performance. This includes analyzing all feedback and creating actions that need to be taken. Team performance should be continuously monitored to ensure that the action actually resulted in improved performance as expected. Techniques that will provide feedback include the Gemba Walk, Evaluation, Review, and Kamishibai Board.

Ceremonies/Techniques

- Gemba Walk

  Leaders can see for themselves the changes that teams have made based on observations and actions. Provide coaching and feedback where needed.

- Evaluation

  Use more formal evaluations to evaluate improvements.

- Review

  Review all the improvement-related feedback with the team to maintain openness and transparency.

- Kamishibai Board

  Use the new or updated cards for the Kamishibai Board to have the agile team do self-checks and make adjustments as needed.

CHAPTER 7

Performance Circle: Teaming

The Teaming performance circle describes actions, roles, and outcomes that address agile teaming (Figure 7-1). Agile leaders have an opportunity to model the successes of agile teams throughout the organization through observation and adoption of common agile ceremonies that may be foreign to team members within the technology, marketing, operations, finance, infrastructure, and purchasing organizations.

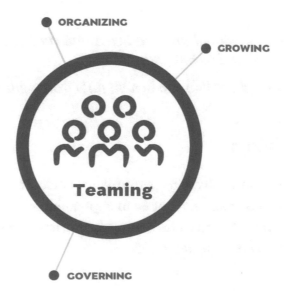

Figure 7-1. *Performance Circle: Teaming*

© Jeff Dalton 2019
J. Dalton, *Great Big Agile*, https://doi.org/10.1007/978-1-4842-4206-3_7

Agile leaders should:

- Employ agile team agreements that align with values across all leadership and organizations.

- Conduct regular retrospectives throughout their organization, and beyond the development team, to identify successes and improvements.

- Deploy coaching and mentoring beyond development teams.

- Adopt visual information management techniques throughout the organization.

- Clearly separate roles from titles and job descriptions.

- Strive for a ceremony-based, high-trust culture that embraces agile values.

Objective

As an agile leader,

I want teams and functional areas to learn and master self-organization and agile ceremonies and techniques,

So that the entire organization can benefit fully from agile adoption.

Holon: Organizing

Organizing is a holon within the Teaming performance circle. The Organizing holon contains the actions and ceremonies required to implement self-organization, interface with non-agile teams, and define the roles of project managers, product owners, and for other roles not defined by any agile framework.

Objective

As an agile leader,

I want to support an agile infrastructure of people, processes, and tools,

So that agile teams have everything needed to be successful.

Performance Level Outcomes

The Organizing holon has the following outcomes defined at each performance level. An organization can achieve performance outcomes by performing the actions and behaviors associated with the specific performance levels (see Table 7-1).

Table 7-1. *Organizing Performance Level Outcomes*

Adopting Level Outcomes	Transforming Level Outcomes	Mastering Level Outcomes
1. Physical space and culture are conducive to team collaboration, communication and focus.	5. Teams establish charters consistent with the culture and values of the agile organization.	9. Teams self-organize based on the organizational agile culture defined, and leaders can measure performance.
2. Teams have the right mix of cross-functional experience necessary to support agile development.	6. Ceremonies and techniques are available to all projects.	10. Projects optimize performance using accessible tools and techniques that are visible organizationally.
3. Teams establish standards and ground rules.	7. Teams begin to own their agile environment.	11. Agile teams integrate or synchronize with other teams and groups as needed to become a Team of Teams.
4. Teams clearly establish roles and accountabilities.	8. Team environments reflect agile values.	

Action 1.0: Establish Agile Team Environments

Develop a work environment that supports our agile values, like *Focus, Collaboration, Humor, Openness*. The physical environment will promote recruitment, retention, performance, creativity, and quality of life. Mixed spaces provide fluidity between collaboration, communication, privacy, and focused development.

Ceremonies/Techniques

- Agile Digs

  Use Agile Digs to create "neighborhoods" in the workspace that allow team space for group work, and space for individual work. Use the Agile Digs strategy to ensure everyone has a "home-space" that does not have to be booked in advance (e.g., "hoteling"). Fill the space with white boards, charts, visual information indicators, and information radiators.

Action 2.0: Establish Roles and Accountabilities

Develop a shared vision and unified expectations of how the team operates. Team members must know what is expected of them and what they can expect of other team members, stakeholders, and leaders. Roles and accountabilities can be reflected in team charters and organizational value statements. If roles and accountabilities are not clear and supported by all, productivity and creativity will be lost in favor of conflicts, misdirection, failures.

Ceremonies/Techniques

- Roles and Accountabilities Game

    Use the ORR game to gain an understanding of what teams perceive as their roles, and how they define the associated accountabilities for each. Help teams, including leaders and functional group members, self-subscribe to accountabilities.

Action 3.0: Promote Self-Organizing and Cross-Functional Teams

Establish an infrastructure for self-organization that incorporates and shares best practices, lessons learned, and process improvements throughout the community. Provide clear visual information to ensure a common vision and true transparency. Observe people and places in action to verify agile values and opportunities to adapt and improve.

Ceremonies/Techniques

- Shared Vision (Obeya Room)

    Use agile values Obeya Rooms to observe your teams sharing and verify the organizations agile values in a visible and transparent way.

- Gemba

    Use Gemba Walks to see teams in action to understand how well they are living your agile vision.

- Kaizen

  Use Kaizen boards to help teams and the whole organization manage continuous improvement efforts. Use Kaizen to allow all teams and leadership to understand improvement priorities and success.

Holon: Growing

Growing is a holon within the Teaming performance circle. The Growing holon contains the actions and ceremonies required to provide a training, mentoring, and learning environment.

Objective

As an agile leader,

I want to provide a training, mentoring, and a learning environment,

So that teams can take full advantage of agile ceremonies, methods, and techniques.

Performance Level Outcomes

The Growing holon has the following outcomes defined at each performance level. An organization can achieve performance outcomes by performing the actions and behaviors associated with the specific performance levels (see Table 7-2).

Table 7-2. *Growing Performance Level Outcomes*

Adopting Level Outcomes	Transforming Level Outcomes	Mastering Level Outcomes
1. Immediate and future training needs are identified.	4. Team effectiveness is measured.	7. Learning is based on team effectiveness measures.
2. Teams regularly review training status.	5. Training is visible in the team environment.	8. Training is constant, consistent, and readily available.
3. Trained mentors are present to increase team performance.	6. Teams determine training needs.	9. Team member competency is evident and demonstrable.

Action 1.0: Identify Training Needs for Agile Teams

Provide teams the opportunity to identify their training needs and opportunities in real time. Training needs are identified and planned at project initiation, but also may arise during sprint planning, retrospectives, and other ceremonies and activities. Ensure training needs are met by inspecting and adapting to the needs of teams.

Ceremonies/Techniques

- Dot Voting

    Use Dot voting to allow teams and leaders to vote their preferences among a set of choices to gain buy in and acceptance on decisions.

Action 2.0: Develop an Organizational Training Backlog

Develop an Organizational Training Backlog to ensure that training opportunities are assessed, prioritized, and available when needed.

Ceremonies/Techniques

- Product Training Backlog

  Use the training product backlog to develop a prioritized list of organizational training needs and to allow resources to contribute to the list. Training backlogs help organizations track and deliver the necessary training that teams crave.

Action 3.0: Establish a Mentoring Program

Establish a hands-on coaching/mentoring program to promote agile values and share best practices from training and process-related experiences. Provide expert coaches and mentors in real-time agile development environments to get the best return on training investments.

Ceremonies/Techniques

- Arc of Conversation

  Use the Arc of conversation to remove biases and actively "hear" what your teams need to meet the organizations objectives and make the most valuable decisions on training, and process improvements.

Action 4.0: Assess the Effectiveness of Training and Mentoring Programs

Assess the effectiveness of training through visual confirmation, where trainers, mentors, or other stakeholders observe trainees and mentees using new skills and exhibiting desired behaviors. Conduct Training Retrospectives to assess the effectiveness of the training and mentoring program and make improvements.

Ceremonies/Techniques

- Confirmation Retrospectives

  Use Confirmation Retrospectives to observe the training results and allow teams to practice their new skills. Consistent training methods and developing team skills will foster improvements throughout the organization.

- Training Retrospectives

  Use Training Retrospectives to identify what the teams thought went well, what did not go well, and what should be change in the training delivered, before investing further. Using Training Retrospectives ensures you are getting the measurable value expected from your investment.

Holon: Governing

Governing is a holon within the Teaming performance circle. The Governing holon contains the actions and ceremonies required to provide a strong agile governance infrastructure for both product and process performance.

Objective

As an agile leader,

I want to provide a strong agile governance infrastructure for both product and process performance,

So that as the business changes, our agile values remain in alignment.

Performance Level Outcomes

The Governing holon has the following outcomes defined at each performance level. An organization can achieve performance outcomes by performing the actions and behaviors associated with the specific performance levels (see Table 7-3).

Table 7-3. *Governing Performance Level Outcomes*

Adopting Level Outcomes	Transforming Level Outcomes	Mastering Level Outcomes
1. Agile roles and accountabilities are understood by team members. 2. Teams identify improvement opportunities. 3. Agile leaders and team members understand agile values.	4. Team members share roles and accountabilities when needed. 5. Team outputs inform performance and organizational improvements. 6. Team objectives and key results are assessed for alignment with agile values.	7. Roles and accountabilities are flexible to meet current team needs. 8. Agile leaders and development team members collaborate to drive continuous improvement. 9. Agile teams are self-governing and agile leaders encourage and support team governance structures. 10. Team objectives and key results are aligned with core organization-wide agile values.

Action 1.0: Align HR with Requirements for Self-Organizing Teams

Review all Human Resource policies, processes, and procedures to ensure they are aligned with agile values and relevant agile roles and techniques.

Ceremonies/Techniques

- Organizational Roles and Accountabilities Game

  Use the ORR game to gain an understanding of what your teams perceive as their roles and how they define the associated accountabilities for each. Help your HR leaders understand the agile team's roles and align policies and procedures with those roles.

Action 2.0: Clarify Team Structure and Reporting Relationships

Empower teams to develop their own self-organizing rules and guidelines in their team agreements within clearly established organizational parameters.

Ceremonies/Techniques

- State of the Team

  Use a State of the Team meeting to understand what teams have accomplished and need from other teams and leadership. Using State of the Team allows leadership to understand a global view of all teams' status and progress.

Action 3.0: Empower a Cross-Functional Group to Deliver Continuous Performance Improvement

Empower team members and leadership to become agile process owners with accountabilities for the care and feeding of selected agile goals and techniques. Train and provide the owners with guidance to make the techniques better, and let them lead the process improvements and communication of changes to the organization.

Ceremonies/Techniques

- All Hands Raised

  Use the All Hands meetings to promote visibility into your successes, strategy, and to promote your agile culture. Using the All Hands meetings allows leaders to see firsthand the talent of their teams, and to inspire the desired agile values.

Action 4.0: Assess Internal Initiatives to Ensure Alignment with Agile Values of the State

Apply and communicate agile values in real time when observing ceremonies and behaviors. Observe outcomes, deliverables, and behaviors to see that they reflect agile values. When observing, are they transparent, open, fun, focused, collaborative, etc.?

Ceremonies/Techniques

- Retrospectives

  Use retrospectives to identify what the teams thought went well, what did not go well, and what should be changed before making further improvements. Using retrospectives ensures you are getting the measurable value expected from deploying process improvements.

- Gemba Walks

  Use Gemba Walks to see the improvements that teams and agile process owners have made based on observations and actions. Provide coaching and feedback where needed.

PART III

Ceremonies and Techniques

CHAPTER 8

Acceptance Testing

Description

Acceptance testing, also known as User Acceptance Testing (UAT), provides the customer with an opportunity to validate that the product increment or released system is able to handle real-life scenarios and transactions. Some of this can be addressed in Sprint Demos/Reviews, but often systems become so complicated that more formal acceptance testing is required. To get the most valuable feedback, testing should be performed by an actual end user, or qualified designate, and should be conducted on the production system in the actual or simulated production environment. The goals of UAT include gaining the customer's approval of the system or product and clearly identifying any defects or issues, and capturing changes to existing use cases or user stories.

© Jeff Dalton 2019
J. Dalton, *Great Big Agile*, https://doi.org/10.1007/978-1-4842-4206-3_8

Typical Roles

- Customer
- End User
- Product Owner
- Scrum Master
- Team Member

Desired Behaviors

1. Conduct UAT at least once in the product development cycle. UAT can be performed during Sprint Reviews and/or at the conclusion of planned releases.

2. Engage one or more end users to perform the testing.

   a. If an end user is not available, have another customer do the testing.

   b. If the customer is not available, have the product owner do the testing.
   Note: The risk of not having an end user or customer participate in testing is that the user community may identify defects after product delivery.

3. Agree upon the test procedures and acceptance criteria before UAT begins.

4. Understand usability problems and any desired changes by having the development team observe the testing activities.

5. Document defects and desired changes. Relate defects and changes to user stories or use cases.

CHAPTER 9

Agile Agreement

Description

An agile agreement is a contract that exists between an agile organization and an agile supplier. While entering into contracts is not new, aligning supplier contracts with agile product development is a contemporary concept. A traditional supplier contract is a low-trust, command-and-control artifact that relies on milestones and deliverables to manage the contract and process payment. An agile agreement is different in that it requires a high-trust, iterative, and incremental approach to supplier management. An agile agreement defines the agile terms and conditions for both parties, the fixed product development time period, and the variable scope of work that the supplier will perform.

© Jeff Dalton 2019
J. Dalton, *Great Big Agile*, https://doi.org/10.1007/978-1-4842-4206-3_9

Typical Roles

- Agile Leader
- Agile Supplier
- Procurement Department
- Product Owner

Desired Behaviors

1. Understand agile values and embed them in the agile agreement.

2. Negotiate with the agile supplier, giving consideration to the following:

   a. Transparency

   b. Collaboration

   c. Failing fast

   d. Iterative and incremental delivery

   e. Risk

   f. Stakeholder Engagement

   g. Scope

   h. Release schedule

3. Continue negotiations until the contract terms and conditions are agreeable to all parties.

4. Document values, contract terms, conditions, and deliverables. For example, adopt a shared definition of done with the agile supplier to enable easier acceptance of deliverables.

5. Execute an agreement so that work can begin. This includes conducting regular retrospectives with the agile supplier to inspect and adapt performance.

6. Monitor and maintain the agile agreement until it is fulfilled or terminated. This involves providing feedback to the procurement department that can be used to select and engage future agile suppliers.

CHAPTER 10

Agile Digs

Description

Agile digs describe the physical or virtual workspace that a leader provides for an agile team. Agile digs is a work environment that aligns with agile values such as collaboration and visibility. To promote collaboration, the workspace enables team members to talk freely, see one another, and gather together in common spaces. To enable visibility, agile digs include wall space, whiteboards, and information radiators. The ideal agile digs environment is a mixed-media space that allows for team collaboration, customer engagement, and individual work.

Leaders should discuss environmental requirements with each team to determine what works for them, and let teams determine the best solutions. Leaders can then implement and guide improvements to ensure the best environment for each team.

© Jeff Dalton 2019
J. Dalton, *Great Big Agile*, https://doi.org/10.1007/978-1-4842-4206-3_10

Typical Roles

- Agile Leader
- Agile Team
- Facilities Manager

Desired Behaviors

1. Review the current physical space and validate that it reflects the following values:

   a. Collaboration

   b. Focus

   c. Transparency

   d. Visibility

2. Seek input from teams for their desired work environment.

3. Identify any impediments in the current work environment, for example, facilities policies, noise, furniture, physical space.

4. Prioritize workspace improvements, with the team's input, based on value and constraints, for example, cost, time, building, furniture.

5. Determine the required visual information management tools, for example, white boards, information radiators, screens, and signs.

6. Make iterative and incremental changes to the team's agile digs.

7. Try it and don't be afraid to fail! You can always improve the team workspace again.

CHAPTER 11

Agile Partner Assessment

Description

The purpose of an Agile Partner Assessment is to select an external partner to collaborate with that is committed to agile values and to deliver products and services in an iterative, incremental way. It is important to carefully analyze and select an agile partner who aligns with your organization. In order to make an informed decision, start with reviewing the organizational agile values and identifying criteria that must be met. Next, conduct research to identify multiple companies that can be evaluated. Last, ensure that key stakeholders are included in making a final selection.

© Jeff Dalton 2019
J. Dalton, *Great Big Agile*, https://doi.org/10.1007/978-1-4842-4206-3_11

Typical Roles

- Agile Leader

- Team Member

- Product Owner

- Procurement Department

- Agile Partner

Desired Behaviors

1. Review project, product, or service requirements for an agile partner.

2. Determine what criteria must be met for selection. Criteria should be weighted as necessary, and an evaluation of agile values should be considered.

3. Select which qualitative or quantitative method will be used to make the selection.

4. Identify multiple agile partners to be considered.

5. Compare agile partners against the criteria. If appropriate, request a demonstration or observe the partners in action to collect performance data.

6. Collaborate with key stakeholders to review comparison results.

7. Select an agile partner.

8. Develop and execute an agile agreement.

CHAPTER 12

All Hands Raised

Description

The purpose of All Hands Raised is for formal and informal leaders to share goals and objectives with teams and functional groups, and more importantly, receive feedback and proactive acknowledgment. As the number and size of teams increase, All Hands Raised provides a structured, yet agile, framework for the sharing of vision and goals, responding to direct questions, and listening to the voice of the organization. The All Hands Raised also helps prevent the corporate version of the "telephone game" wherein important messaging is diluted and transformed beyond recognition.

© Jeff Dalton 2019
J. Dalton, *Great Big Agile*, https://doi.org/10.1007/978-1-4842-4206-3_12

Typical Roles

- Agile Leader

- Agile Team

- Product Owner

- Scrum Master

- Program Manager

- Agile Partner

- Business Customer

Desired Behaviors

1. Develop a regular schedule for All Hands Raised events to be held at least biannually.

2. Request input from teams prior to the event, including what teams need to be successful, and impediments they are experiencing.

3. Meet in a common area that allows teams to see and hear leadership directly.

4. Do not try to solve problems during the All Hands Raised meeting. Use it simply to communicate information and listen.

5. Create a backlog of ideas and improvement suggestions gathered at the meeting.

6. Have fun and get to know your organization!

CHAPTER 13

Arc of Conversation

Description

The Arc of Conversation is a communication framework used to resolve a concern or overcome an impediment. It involves coaching and active listening from one party and honest, direct communication from the other party. The key to the arc of conversation is for the "coach" to provide a comfortable environment for the "coachee" to speak their mind. The desired results of this communication framework are a common understanding of the issues, identification of possible solutions, and a shared accountability for the resulting actions.

© Jeff Dalton 2019
J. Dalton, *Great Big Agile*, https://doi.org/10.1007/978-1-4842-4206-3_13

Typical Roles

- Coach

- Coachee

- Scrum Master

- Team Member

Desired Behaviors

1. Select a neutral, private location for the conversation to take place.

2. Keep the conversation positive.

3. Keep moving forward, and do not dwell on any one comment or issue.

4. Beginning: Start the conversation

    a. Open the conversation with words and body language that create a comfortable space.

    b. Invite coachee to express their concerns openly without judgment or consequences.

    c. Provide room for the coachee to speak, vent, and explain.

    d. Practice active listening and empathy.

5. Middle: Ask questions

    a. Ask the coachee questions that inspire thought and insight.

    b. Ask questions that help the coachee to reach their own conclusions without leading them to predetermined outcomes.

    c. Do not attempt to solve the problem at this stage of the conversation.

6. End: Support the outcome

    a. Once the coachee has chosen the action to take, support them by defining accountabilities for any actions to be taken.

    b. Thank the coachee for their trust and openness, and invite them to participate in similar conversations in the future.

CHAPTER 14

Automated Build

Description

Automated Build is a component of an overall continuous integration or continuous build strategy that increases product quality and development efficiency. Automated Build is a system that executes unit and regression testing on completed code modules without manual intervention, checks the modules into a configuration management (code management) system, compiles them, and, assuming success, builds them into the larger code base for integration, system, and user acceptance testing. An automated build system can also enforce rules, such as coding standards, and improve code quality using success criteria.

© Jeff Dalton 2019
J. Dalton, *Great Big Agile*, https://doi.org/10.1007/978-1-4842-4206-3_14

Typical Roles

- Team Member

- Chief Engineer

- Software Architect

Desired Behaviors

1. Establish common coding standards for formatting, naming, intra-application interfaces, APIs, and static analysis quality checks.

2. Define rules that regulate check-in of code modules based on standards.

3. Enforce the rules through the build automation.

4. Automate as much unit and integration testing as possible.

5. Use automation to promote code that has passed all automated tests, and block code that has not passed the required tests.

6. Maintain and improve the automated build system.

CHAPTER 15

Backlog Grooming

Description

Backlog grooming (sometimes called *story-time*) is a common technique used by product owners and teams to clarify, size, and prioritize the backlog of epics and user stories before and during a sprint. The product owner has accountability for the product backlog and engages in regular, collaborative discussions with the agile team to review and revise it. The agile team supports backlog grooming by providing knowledge of the product or service being developed and the relative size of the epics and user stories in the backlog. New epics and user stories may emerge as a result of backlog grooming. It is the responsibility of the product owner to capture these within the product backlog along with their acceptance criteria. Backlog grooming typically includes a negotiation between the product owner and the agile team on which user stories will be added, removed, or revised. The user stories at the top of the backlog are typically included in the next sprint or iteration.

Additional backlogs, other than the product backlog, may be groomed to prioritize work items related to continuous improvement or non-product-related activities. In these cases, the stakeholders and frequency of backlog grooming may vary.

© Jeff Dalton 2019
J. Dalton, *Great Big Agile*, https://doi.org/10.1007/978-1-4842-4206-3_15

Typical Roles

- Agile Team
- Business SME (subject matter expert)
- Product Owner

Desired Behaviors

1. Create the initial product backlog by collecting and documenting epics and/or user stories associated with the desired product.

2. Sequence the user stories in the backlog based on business value and priority. The highest priority user stories are at the top of the backlog, and the lowest priority user stories are at the bottom.

3. Review and evaluate the user stories (product owner and agile team) using a defined set of quality criteria (e.g., INVEST (Independent, Negotiable, Valuable, Estimable, Sized, and Testable)).

4. Identify user stories that do not meet the criteria and update them accordingly.

5. Establish or update traceability between epics, user stories, and child user stories.

6. If backlog grooming is occurring mid-sprint, identify the stories that are most likely to be included in the upcoming sprint.

CHAPTER 16

Best Practices Board

Description

A Best Practices Board displays the best ideas, work products, and lessons learned from one or more agile teams, functional group, or manager for the benefit of the entire agile community. Best practices are harvested from retrospectives conducted by agile teams, functional groups, and the enterprise. Defined criteria are used to select best practices that are truly "best in class." Someone is assigned the accountability for posting and maintaining best practices on a physical or virtual board. The Best Practices Board is located in an area that is accessible to all members of the agile community. This could be a white board in a common area, a filterable list in a tool or wiki page, or a large digital screen in each team area.

© Jeff Dalton 2019
J. Dalton, *Great Big Agile*, https://doi.org/10.1007/978-1-4842-4206-3_16

Typical Roles

- Agile Leader
- Team Member
- Scrum Master

Desired Behaviors

1. Determine optimal locations for Best Practices Boards. Ensure that they are in common areas where all teams and groups can access them.

2. Assign at least one person with the role and accountability for updating each Best Practices Board.

3. Communicate the criteria for best practices to all team members and ensure that they are understood.

4. Develop expectations for when best practices are shared, and at what frequency.

5. Ensure that all team members review the relevant Best Practices Boards prior to each project kickoff.

6. Monitor Best Practices Boards to ensure that they meet the established criteria, contain current information, and are used by projects and groups.

7. Team members know where the Best Practices Board is located, and they review it periodically and when initiating new projects.

CHAPTER 17

Big Room Planning / Release Zero

Description

Big Room Planning (Scaled Agile Framework), sometimes called Release Zero (Agile CMMI), is a broadly attended, intensely focused stakeholder event, often lasting for two days or more, where long-term planning, interdependency identification, systems learning, organizational architecture, and the performance and planning framework for a successful program is established.

© Jeff Dalton 2019
J. Dalton, *Great Big Agile*, https://doi.org/10.1007/978-1-4842-4206-3_17

Typical Roles

- Program Sponsor(s)
- Agile Leader(s)
- Team Members
- Scrum Master (s)
- Product Owner(s)
- Systems Architect(s)
- Marketing Team
- Business Development Team

Desired Behaviors

On your mark...

1. Prepare for the event with robust value stream / business process mapping.

2. Develop a draft for an organizational structure that supports and promotes agile values. This could include: governance infrastructure that supports self-organization and relentless, continuous improvement; and a tool-chain that supports as much automation as can be afforded by the organization.

3. Explore and document the organizational capacity and constraints that will impact the program using available productivity data.

Get set...

1. Identify, train, and coach potential leaders at all levels.

2. Ensure all participants and stakeholders, especially leaders, are keenly aware of agile values, frameworks, and techniques, and understand the value of embracing an agile organizational architecture.

3. Develop a product vision, and clearly identify expectations, outcomes, and a definition of done that considers systems, schedule, stakeholders, resources, finances, risks, and issues that should be uncovered and resolved

4. Develop a clear, prioritized planning backlog.

Go!

1. Using the vision, backlog, and organizational capacity as a guide, begin cross-functional planning with the aid of one or more facilitators or scrum masters.

2. See Chapter 72 on Visual Information Management for guidance on sharing all planning, risks, and issues for the entire group to aid in information transference, transparency, and collaboration.

3. See Chapter 41 on Open Space Technology for more information about succeeding in an environment where the outcomes are unclear.

CHAPTER 18

Brainstorming

Description

Brainstorming is a group discussion technique used to generate new ideas or solutions related to a goal or a problem. A brainstorming session has a facilitator who welcomes all ideas and records them as they are offered. Participants quickly and spontaneously state their ideas in a manner that evokes kernels of corn being popped. The group avoids evaluating or critiquing the ideas during the brainstorming session. The facilitator helps the group to avoid planning or determining how the ideas will be implemented. Brainstorming sessions may be time-boxed or terminated when there are no more ideas to offer (or kernels of corn to pop). For a successful brainstorming session, establish ground rules such as:

- Check all titles and authorities at the door.
- Set duration of the brainstorming session.
- Allow no solution engineering, only idea generation.
- Define the follow-up process.

© Jeff Dalton 2019
J. Dalton, *Great Big Agile*, https://doi.org/10.1007/978-1-4842-4206-3_18

Typical Roles

- Agile Leader

- Agile Team

- Scrum Master

- Product Owner

- SME

Desired Behaviors

1. Define the goal, problem statement, or context that will be addressed by the brainstorming session. Communicate it to all participants before they attend the session.

2. Identify and communicate ground rules.

3. Prepare the boards, tools, and supplies that are needed to conduct the Brainstorming session (e.g., sticky notes, markers, flip charts, boards, mind mapping tools, projector).

4. Identify a capable facilitator.

5. Ensure understanding of the goal, problem statement, or context of the session before brainstorming begins.

6. Be open to all ideas.

7. Ask questions to invite new ideas and involve all participants.

8. Record and display all ideas during the session.

9. Review or summarize all ideas at the end of the session. Identify and assign follow-up actions.

CHAPTER 19

Burn Down Chart

Description

A burn down chart is an information radiator that visually depicts a "value trajectory" of the sprint/iteration. Based on the number of story points an agile team is historically able to "burn down" during each sprint ("velocity"), the burn down chart helps the product owner, agile team, and leadership to understand whether or not they will deliver the desired business value and functionality that was identified in the forecast during sprint/iteration planning.

A burn down chart can be used to monitor value delivered during a sprint or a release. A sprint burn down chart visually depicts the value delivered, and what is remaining in the forecast for the current sprint/iteration. Agile teams that are engaged in multi-sprint releases may also use a release burn down chart to depict progress across all sprints in the release. Release burn down charts are useful for product owners and leadership to understand overall business value delivered, but they require agile teams to have consistent membership and fixed sprint duration for all sprints in the release.

Agile teams may also use the burn up chart, which depicts similar data, but is oriented toward what is yet to be completed rather than what has been delivered.

© Jeff Dalton 2019
J. Dalton, *Great Big Agile*, https://doi.org/10.1007/978-1-4842-4206-3_19

Typical Roles

- Agile Leader
- Product Owner
- Agile Team

Desired Behaviors

1. The source for the story points on the y-axis (vertical axis) in the burn down chart comes from the sprint forecast. This is the total number of story points for the user stories that the agile team committed to for this sprint.

2. Use story points, not hours or days, to indicate value delivered or work accomplished.

3. Update the burn down chart at the end of each day, or during the daily stand-up meeting.

4. Place the duration of the sprint/iteration along the x-axis (horizontal axis) in the burn down chart.

5. Use the burn down chart throughout the sprint to understand how much work (or value) the agile team has accomplished so far and how much work (or value) remains to be done.

CHAPTER 20

Confirmation

Description

User stories have three critical components often called the 3Cs: card, conversation, and confirmation. User stories are often written on cards, or a digital equivalent. The card does not contain all the information, but is a reminder of what the story is about for the requirements discovery and backlog grooming ceremony. The detail about each requirement, epic, or story is communicated from the product owner to the agile team through conversation that involves an exchange of views, scenarios, and operational workflow. The product owner typically defines the confirmation, or acceptance criteria, directly before user stories are selected for each sprint.

Communication of the confirmation criteria to the agile team ensures that the team and the product owner have a shared understanding of the product's features and functions. The product owner may also capture confirmation criteria in acceptance tests that are performed for each user story. When the acceptance tests yield passing results, it confirms to the customer that the associated user story is truly done.

© Jeff Dalton 2019
J. Dalton, *Great Big Agile*, https://doi.org/10.1007/978-1-4842-4206-3_20

Typical Roles

- Scrum Team

- Product Owner

- Stakeholder

- Scrum Master

Desired Behaviors

1. Specific acceptance criteria (definition of done) is established for each user story.

2. The acceptance criteria is shared with, and agreed to, by the team.

3. The product owner confirms that each story is complete before it can be considered "done."

4. All acceptance tests are in a passing state before product or service is delivered.

CHAPTER 21

Continuous Deployment

Description

Continuous Deployment is an extension of continuous integration, and it is focused on minimizing the time between product development and that product being used by end users. Continuous deployment is the process that takes validated features from continuous integration and deploys them into the production environment where they are tested and prepared for release. The goal is to deliver incremental and valuable solutions to the end users as frequently as possible. To enable continuous deployment, the team typically relies on automation tools.

© Jeff Dalton 2019
J. Dalton, *Great Big Agile*, https://doi.org/10.1007/978-1-4842-4206-3_21

Typical Roles

- Scrum Team

- Product Owner

- Scrum Master

- Stakeholder

Desired Behaviors

1. Maintain development and testing environments to match the production environment as closely as possible.

2. Build a staging environment that replicates the production environment.

3. Deploy validated code to the staging environment after each iteration.

4. Automate the testing of the features and system functionality.

5. Deploy the infrastructure and supporting code structure to automate deployment.

CHAPTER 22

Continuous Integration

Description

Continuous Integration (CI) refers to the assembly of product components in incremental stages, using a purposeful strategy and defined procedures. CI integration is an approach to continuous testing and product integration that was first introduced in extreme programming (XP), but is now common in almost all successful agile projects. In a CI environment, an application is built and unit tested, and in some cases integration tested, using automated tools, each time new code is "checked-in" to the code management system.

J. Dalton, *Great Big Agile*, https://doi.org/10.1007/978-1-4842-4206-3_22

Typical Roles

- Configuration Manager (typically for larger teams)

- Team Member

Desired Behaviors

1. Set up a code repository for configuration management.

2. Build servers and scripts to automate the integration and testing of checked-in code configured to build and compile the application at frequent intervals.

3. Commit code to the baseline repository as it is completed to enforce early integration testing.

4. Run automated unit and integration tests at frequent intervals.

5. Publish and review the results.

CHAPTER 23

Class, Responsibilities, Collaborators (CRC) Cards

Description

CRC Cards (Class, Responsibilities, Collaborators) are typically used when object-oriented design and development is preferred, and are helpful when there is a need to rapidly design one or more product features that may be instantiated as an object within the source code. First, two or more team members write down the names of the most critical classes involved in the feature on index cards. Second, the cards are fleshed out with lists of the responsibilities of each class and the names of collaborators (i.e., other dependent classes). Third, team members perform a role-playing exercise and assume the role of one or more classes while playing out a plausible scenario of the design.

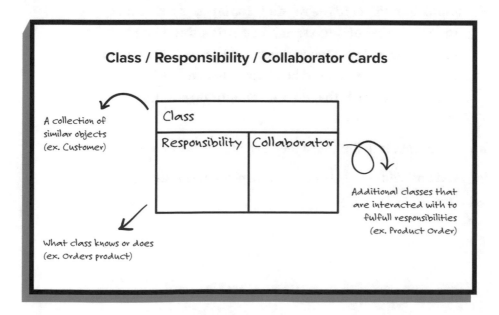

© Jeff Dalton 2019
J. Dalton, *Great Big Agile*, https://doi.org/10.1007/978-1-4842-4206-3_23

Typical Roles

- Agile Team

- Product Owner

- Business SME

Desired Behaviors

1. Identify the core classes that are the building blocks of the product. Look for the nouns in the design documentation to identify three-to-five main classes.

2. Create one index card per class (begin with class names only).

3. Add responsibilities for each class by looking for the verbs in the design documentation. Ask yourself: "What does a class do? What information needs to be maintained?"

4. Determine dependencies with other classes. A class often does not have sufficient information to fulfill its responsibilities. Therefore, it must collaborate (work) with other classes to get the job done.

5. Reposition the cards as needed. To improve the team's understanding of the system, the cards should be placed on the table in an intuitive manner. Two cards that collaborate with one another should be placed close together on the table, whereas two cards that do not collaborate should be placed far apart.

6. Move classes to the side if they become unnecessary.

7. Add and refine until everyone on the team is satisfied.

CHAPTER 24

Daily Stand-Up

Description

The Daily Stand-Up (or "Daily Scrum" or "Daily Meeting") is an agile technique that is popular with most agile teams. It is used to maintain a shared understanding of progress, identify impediments and risks early ("fail fast"), and increase collaboration and transparency among team members. As the name indicates, the meeting occurs every day, and participants often stand for the duration of the meeting in order to encourage brevity.

There are primarily two approaches to conducting a Daily Stand-Up meeting. The first is to conduct a meeting where information is provided based on the active user stories for the current sprint. The other method, known as "round-robin," is used to share information related to current tasks, forecast, and any impediments each team member may have.

The Daily Stand-Up meeting is usually facilitated by the scrum master and involves all agile team members. Depending on the maturity of the team, and the level of trust with product owners and other stakeholders, it may be useful to include extended team members, but typical attendees are those who are performing tasks related to the goal of the current sprint.

© Jeff Dalton 2019
J. Dalton, *Great Big Agile*, https://doi.org/10.1007/978-1-4842-4206-3_24

Typical Roles

- Scrum Master

- Agile Team

- Product Owner (optional)

- Extended Team Members (optional)

Desired Behaviors

1. Conduct the Daily Stand-Up at the same time each day in order to decrease complexity.

2. Hold the meeting face to face, if possible, or using virtual technology if face to face is not possible.

3. The scrum master facilitates the workflow of the meeting.

4. Timebox the Daily Stand-Up to 15 minutes or less.

5. Each team member shares:

    a. What was completed since the last Daily Stand-Up.

    b. What is planned for completion today.

    c. What issues or risks are impeding progress.

6. With large teams, consider the use of a "token" to identify the team member who is speaking.

7. The scrum master records the impediments, risks, and issues that are identified during the meeting.

8. The scrum master works to remove impediments, reduce risks, and resolve issues outside of the Daily Stand-Up meeting.

CHAPTER 25

Definition of Done

Description

The definition of done (DOD) is a fundamental element of any agile project that helps maintain quality and limit scope. It is an agreement within the team that defines what must be completed for each user story in order to be presented at a sprint review with the product owner. Definition of done can be applied to epics, user stories, and tasks using unique criteria to define when each is "done." The DOD can be extended to each agile including sprint planning, sprint demos, retrospectives, and backlog grooming in order to achieve team agreement that each ceremony is complete. In that case, the DOD defines the tasks and work items required to complete each agile ceremony.

Definition of Done Examples:

- Code and test cases are written.

- Code was peer reviewed and met coding standards.

- Code passed all relevant unit tests.

- User story was tested and passed all associated tests.

- Code was deployed to system test environment and passed system tests.

- Code was deployed to integration environment and passed integration tests.

- User story/test cases passed User Acceptance Testing (UAT). The UAT is based on the acceptance criteria that were established for the user story.

© Jeff Dalton 2019
J. Dalton, *Great Big Agile*, https://doi.org/10.1007/978-1-4842-4206-3_25

- The remaining hours for a task are set to zero and a user story is moved to "Done" on the scrum board.

- Required product documentation (e.g., User Guide, Installation Guide, design documents) was produced, reviewed, and approved.

- Any build, deployment, or configuration changes were implemented, documented, and communicated.

Typical Roles

- Agile Team
- Product Owner

Desired Behaviors

1. Convene the team and agree on which work products and ceremonies will be subject to the definition of done.

2. Convene the agile team to establish and agree upon the definition of done for a typical user story, and any other work product subject to the DOD.

3. Post the DOD as an information radiator in a location visible to all team members.

4. Use the DOD to determine if each user story or work product is complete before moving it to the "Done" column on the task board.

5. Discuss the effectiveness of the team's DOD at each sprint retrospective. Adjust the DOD as necessary.

CHAPTER 26

Definition of Ready

Description

A definition of ready (DOR) enables a team to specify certain preconditions that must be met before a user story can be accepted into a sprint. The goal of the DOR is to identify defects in the story before work has commenced, thereby reducing defects early, when they are the least costly to address. User stories that are "ready" are clear, concise, sized appropriately for a sprint, and most importantly, actionable.

© Jeff Dalton 2019
J. Dalton, *Great Big Agile*, https://doi.org/10.1007/978-1-4842-4206-3_26

Typical Roles

1. Agile Team

2. Product Owner

3. Scrum Master

Desired Behaviors

1. Develop a checklist to outline the criteria for the agile team's definition of ready.

2. Apply the INVEST (or other) criteria to ensure that a user story is Independent, Negotiable, Valuable, Estimable, Sized appropriately, and Testable.

3. Avoid rules that require full compliance to DOR at all times, allowing for exceptions based on specific attributes of the user story.

4. Post the definition of ready in the location visible to all team members.

5. Use the definition of ready during the sprint planning meeting to determine if user stories can be accepted into the sprint backlog.

6. Discuss the effectiveness of the team's definition of ready at the sprint retrospective. Adjust as the team becomes more aware of what makes up a good, actionable user story.

CHAPTER 27

Dot Voting

Description

Dot Voting is a technique that allows an agile team to quickly select or prioritize items with input from all team members. Each team member is given the same number of dot stickers and instructed to place the stickers near the list of items they wish to select or prioritize. Team members may place as many dots as they wish on any item(s) on the list. Items with the most dots are selected or prioritized based on the number of dots they receive. This technique is frequently used during the sprint retrospective to help prioritize improvements.

© Jeff Dalton 2019
J. Dalton, *Great Big Agile*, https://doi.org/10.1007/978-1-4842-4206-3_27

Typical Roles

1. Agile Team

2. Scrum Master

3. Product Owner

Desired Behaviors

1. Post the options (e.g., user stories, items, solutions, improvements) on the wall using sticky notes, flip charts, or other visible medium.

2. Explain the goal of the session (e.g., select the best alternative, rank order user stories) and why each vote is important. Discuss the options and answer any questions from participants.

3. Give the same number of dots to each participant. Alternatively, a marker may be used so the team member can record their vote directly on the sticky note or flip chart.

4. Ask the participants to vote by placing their dots. Participants should apply dots under or beside the items they prioritize.

5. Count the votes and announce the items with the highest number of votes. If ranking is required, rank order the items from the most number of dots to the least.

6. Briefly discuss the items that were selected or prioritized the highest. If the participants are not in agreement with the voting outcome, take the following action:

   a. Arrange the votes into three groups to represent high, medium, and low priorities.

   b. Discuss the items in each group.

   c. Move items around to create a high-priority list.

   d. Take a new vote with items in the high-priority list.

CHAPTER 28

Epics

Description

An epic is a large user story that describes a body of work that cannot be completed in a single sprint. Teams will break down an epic into smaller user stories that can be accepted and completed within a single sprint. The product owner has responsibility for writing epics and the user stories that result from them. Both epics and user stories are maintained in the product backlog.

Sprint allocation is not the only reason to break down an epic. Customers often request features that are complex and that need to be broken down into smaller components to be understood and implemented by the team. These epics need to be subdivided into smaller user stories. If a user story requires more than one agile team to complete the work, the story would be considered an epic, as this story will need to be divided into at least two user stories, one for each agile team.

© Jeff Dalton 2019
J. Dalton, *Great Big Agile*, https://doi.org/10.1007/978-1-4842-4206-3_28

Typical Roles

- Agile Team
- Product Owner

Desired Behaviors

1. Epics are identified during initial product visioning, release planning, or backlog grooming. The product owner records epics and adds them to the product backlog.

2. Epics are broken down into user stories during backlog grooming, sprint planning, or other regular team events. The breakdown process is often iterative and involves the product owner and the agile team.

3. Agile frameworks have no standard measurement for what makes a user story an epic, although it is commonly understood that an epic can span multiple sprints, but a user story must be contained in one.

CHAPTER 29

Evaluation

Description

Evaluation is a method to understand how work is being done. Whereas a Gemba Walk is to "go and see," an evaluation is to ask, record, and provide feedback to an agile team or functional group. Evaluations are conducted against a known baseline, and they are performed by an objective, trained resource using a checklist or commonly understood set of criteria. Results are communicated to the agile team or functional group to help them improve team performance. Evaluations are valuable for understanding the consistency of behaviors across many teams within a large organization.

© Jeff Dalton 2019
J. Dalton, *Great Big Agile*, https://doi.org/10.1007/978-1-4842-4206-3_29

Typical Roles

- Evaluator (e.g., agile leader, agile team member, scrum master)
- Agile Team

Desired Behaviors

1. Evaluations are conducted against a defined standard or common set of expectations.

2. All participants are made aware of both the content and timing of evaluations.

3. The evaluator gathers useful information that can help improve the team, group, or organization.

4. Individual team members are not evaluated. Evaluations are conducted on teams or functional groups only.

5. Foster an environment where everyone is able to evaluate an organization, group, or team that is independent from their own. This may involve establishing an evaluator role that rotates periodically among different people in the organization.

6. Add improvements and impediments discovered during evaluations to the appropriate backlogs.

7. Evaluators follow up with the agile team or functional group to verify that improvements were considered appropriately.

CHAPTER 30

Frequent Releases

Description

Frequent Releases is a looser and more relaxed version of Continuous Deployment. Their primary purpose is to put new or updated products into the hands of the end-user community quickly to gather feedback and respond rapidly to change requests. A release plan is used to define the frequency and timing of releases, and they can occur after each sprint or on a calendar schedule. Monthly releases that include the product increments of two two-week sprints are common among large agile organizations.

J. Dalton, *Great Big Agile*, https://doi.org/10.1007/978-1-4842-4206-3_30

Typical Roles

- Agile Team
- Product Owner

Desired Behaviors

1. Develop a frequent release plan. Include the agile team(s) and any other roles that are responsible for development and deployment in the creation of the frequent release plan.

2. Define the timing of each release.

3. Groom and define the epic and user story content of the next two to three releases.

4. Keep the frequent release plan up to date.

5. Display the frequent release plan in the agile team's workspace using visual information management systems.

CHAPTER 31

Gemba Walks

Description

A Gemba Walk is a technique used to observe and understand how work is being performed. Gemba is taken from the Japanese word *gembutsu*, meaning "real thing" or "real place," and a Gemba Walk has the following elements: observation (watching people perform work in-person); location (observing people at the actual location where work is performed); teaming (interacting with people performing the work). Gemba Walks provide an up-close, detailed view of behaviors in action and are a powerful tool for identifying process improvement opportunities and new ways to support the agile team. They are also useful methods for leaders to see how agile teams are demonstrating agile values.

J. Dalton, *Great Big Agile*, https://doi.org/10.1007/978-1-4842-4206-3_31

Typical Roles

- Agile Leader

- Scrum Master

- Agile Coach

- Agile Team or Functional Group

Desired Behaviors

1. Gemba Walks are performed at the location where work activities occur.

2. Observe teams while they work, and ask questions if appropriate.

3. Understand the workers' perspectives on how the work is performed, including their view of problems and improvement suggestions.

4. Do not use the Gemba Walk to solve problems.

5. Record observations and improvement opportunities.

6. Provide timely feedback to the team or functional group.

CHAPTER 32

Gemba Kaizen

Gemba Kaizen is a Japanese concept of continuous improvement designed for enhancing processes. Gemba refers to the location where work is performed, while Kaizen is tied to the improvements. Gemba Kaizen includes identifying changes, making improvements, monitoring changes, and readjusting as necessary. An individual, group of people, or an improvement suggestion system can perform Kaizen. Having a strategic system in place to monitor improvements will lead to great results in the long-term overall improvement.

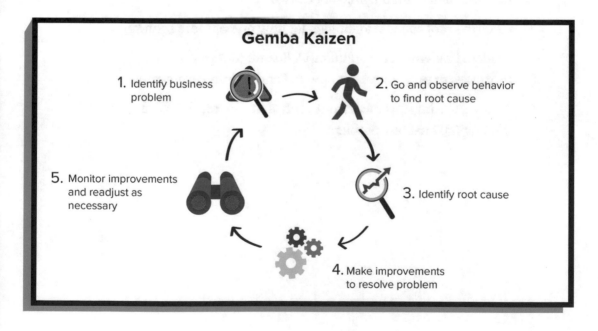

Gemba Kaizen

1. Identify business problem
2. Go and observe behavior to find root cause
3. Identify root cause
4. Make improvements to resolve problem
5. Monitor improvements and readjust as necessary

© Jeff Dalton 2019
J. Dalton, *Great Big Agile*, https://doi.org/10.1007/978-1-4842-4206-3_32

Typical Roles

- Agile CXO
- Agile Leader
- Agile Team

Desired Behaviors

1. Identify business problems that are recognized by the organization.

2. Observe the known problem using a Gemba Walk.

3. Identify the root cause. Use of lean techniques such as "five why's" can be useful in identifying root causes.

4. Once the root cause is identified, identify one or more solutions.

5. Work to implement the solution(s). Ensure that all necessary processes or procedures are updated and training is provided.

6. Monitor the improvements and verify that the solution addressed the original business problem.

CHAPTER 33

Goal, Question, Metric (GQM)

Description

Goal, Question, Metric (GQM) is an approach developed in the early 1980s, piloted at the NASA Goddard Space Flight Center; it is used to derive useful measurements from one or more goals.

- Goals are established based on an organization's or team's mission, vision, strategic goals, and improvement objectives.

- One or more questions are identified for each goal to refine the goal into information needs.

- One or more metrics are identified to answer each question.

- Metrics are selected and related back to the goals to ensure that they measure goal attainment and progress.

One advantage of GQM is that it provides traceability between what is being measured and the goals that are important to an organization or a team. This traceability focuses measurement activities on metrics that are useful and valuable, and eliminates measurement overhead. Knowing whether there is a return on investment for goals and initiatives creates a culture of continuous improvement and an entrepreneurial, "fail fast" mindset for individuals.

© Jeff Dalton 2019
J. Dalton, *Great Big Agile*, https://doi.org/10.1007/978-1-4842-4206-3_33

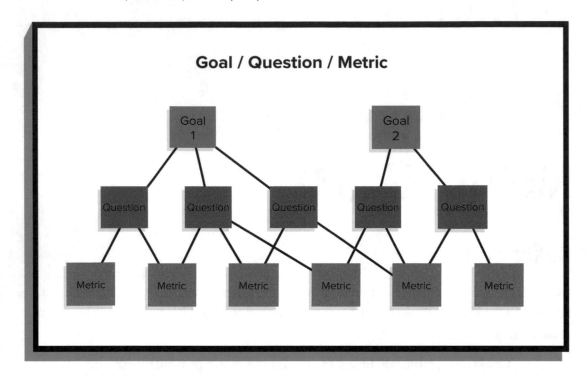

Typical Roles

- Agile Leader
- Agile Team
- Managers
- Product Owner
- Scrum Master

Desired Behaviors

1. Employ a trained GQM facilitator to plan and manage GQM sessions.

2. Involve multiple levels of the organization to create measurable goals, the right questions, and useful metrics.

3. In order to be successful, be willing to invest in systems and tools that provide data that is needed, not just what is currently available.

4. Define the smallest set of metrics possible to measure achievement of the most important goals first.

5. Display data and progress using visual information management systems.

6. Do not create metrics that punish or embarrass individual performers (shaming is not an agile value).

7. Regularly inspect and adapt the measurement program to fail fast and continually improve.

CHAPTER 34

Incremental Development

Description

Incremental Development is the practice of breaking the delivery of features or functions into small pieces that can be envisioned, built, tested, and delivered in a predictable, timeboxed period of time. Through the completion of multiple increments, a working system is created and delivered that fulfills the functional and nonfunctional requirements. The approach requires multidiscipline engagement, and the creation of a design and other documentation in matching increments. Paired with Iterative Development, it is a powerful and predictable work management system that forms the basis of most agile frameworks.

J. Dalton, *Great Big Agile*, https://doi.org/10.1007/978-1-4842-4206-3_34

Typical Roles

- Product Owner
- Agile Team
- Scrum Master

Desired Behaviors

1. Include the team(s) responsible for development and delivery of the product in the creation of the incremental development plan.

2. Break up the planned functionality into the smallest possible increments.

3. Keep the plan, designs, and other documentation current with each iteration.

4. Inspect and adapt the plan as learning occurs during each increment.

5. Display the plan using visual information management systems.

CHAPTER 35

Kamishibai (Board and Cards)

Description

A Kamishibai Board is a visual information management system used to plan and capture the results of process audits on the most critical processes in the organization. The primary purpose is to give leaders a schedule for when to audit a process and what behaviors to observe. A Kamishibai Board is often part of the Gemba, the location where work is performed. The board shows the status and results of the required audits for each team or group and displays notes about issues, risks, and corrective actions. The primary goal of the board is to enable immediate problem resolution.

Kamishibai Cards, also known as "T-cards," are used to define, allocate, and visualize process level audits carried out by project managers (or team leaders) and leaders who are one or two levels above in the organizational governance structure. The T-cards are randomly selected from a box by a leader so that the checks are random.

© Jeff Dalton 2019
J. Dalton, *Great Big Agile*, https://doi.org/10.1007/978-1-4842-4206-3_35

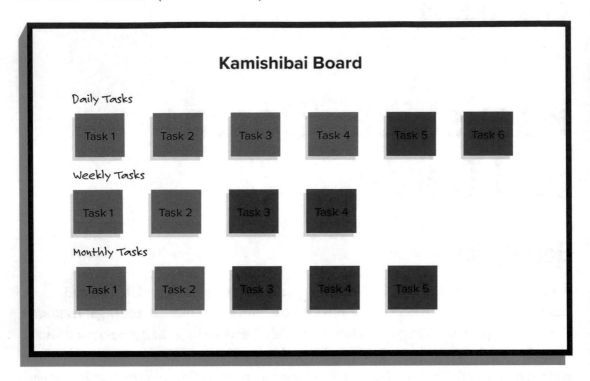

Typical Roles

- Agile Leader
- Project Manager
- Team Leader
- Leadership Team

Desired Behaviors

1. Determine which processes, changes, or improvements are most important to the team or organization. These will become the focus of the Kamishibai checks.

2. Identify the agile teams, projects, or groups for the checks (or process audits).

3. Assign an agile leader to each team, project, or group to conduct the audit.

4. Create the initial set of T-cards.

5. Deploy the Kamishibai boards to each team or group.

6. Define expectations for how often the checks are done, and who is required to do them.

7. Add Kamishibai as part of Gemba Walks.

8. Ensure that a coaching, learning, and improvement culture resulting from Kamishibai checks is maintained.

CHAPTER 36

Kanban Board

Description

A Kanban Board is a visual work management system that enables understanding and optimization of continuous work being performed by a team or functional group. The board depicts the state of work across the top, and the flow of work as it goes through each state. A basic Kanban Board has states for "waiting," "in progress," and "completed." Teams are free to adapt the board and can define as many states as needed to understand how much work is to be done, being done, and is done. A major goal of Kanban is to limit work in progress to drive improvements in efficiency and throughput. Choose Kanban when the work in the "waiting" state is not easily predictable, or when the type of work is driven by demand.

Kanban works well in many settings, and it is popular with teams that do application support and maintenance activities.

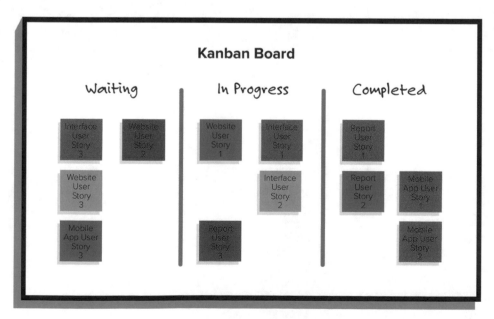

© Jeff Dalton 2019
J. Dalton, *Great Big Agile*, https://doi.org/10.1007/978-1-4842-4206-3_36

Typical Roles

- Agile Team

Desired Behaviors

1. Define the desired work states for the Kanban Board.

2. Use visual information management systems to create, maintain, and display the board.

3. Define team rules for limiting the work in progress.

4. Add work to the "waiting" queue.

5. Record basic information, such as the name of each team member who is doing the work in each state, and how much time the work item was in each state.

6. Periodically analyze data from the Kanban Board to make improvements and increase the amount of work that can be "in progress."

CHAPTER 37

Kano Model

Description

The Kano Model is a technique used in product development to identify the most appropriate mix of features in order to maximize the satisfaction of a product. When using the Kano Model, product features are grouped into three categories: Basic, Performance, and Exciters. The Basic category contains features that the product is expected to have. For example, if the product is an automobile, turn signals would be considered a basic feature. These features do not drive satisfaction with the product, but the absence of a Basic feature can lessen customer satisfaction with a product. The Performance category contains features that can drive a linear increase in satisfaction. Features that fall into the Exciter category are the type of features that can differentiate the product and make it stand out from the competition in the market.

The Kano Model also includes an approach for evaluating results from customer surveys. The surveys provide data on the specific product features that are desirable and undesirable to customers. Applying survey results to the Kano Model helps product owners to prioritize product features and make decisions about which features to include in the product backlog.

© Jeff Dalton 2019
J. Dalton, *Great Big Agile*, https://doi.org/10.1007/978-1-4842-4206-3_37

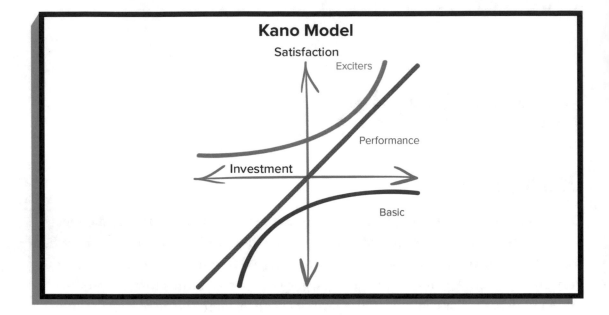

Typical Roles

- Product Owner

- Product Management Team

- Agile Team

Desired Behaviors

1. Product features are categorized as Basic, Performance, or Exciters.

2. Product vision and road map include features that fall into the Performance and Exciter categories.

3. Basic features are included in the product backlog.

4. The Kano Model is used to evaluate customer survey results and customer feedback. Product features are assigned to categories in the model.

5. The product backlog is updated with additional features from the Performance and Exciter categories as determined by the product owner.

CHAPTER 38

Lean Coffee

Description

Lean Coffee is an agile technique that allows for successful, collaborative meetings with minimal planning or agenda setting. Personal Kanban boards, sticky notes, sharpies, and innovative voting techniques such as dot voting, fist-to-five, or even dart-guns with targets are often used to aid in the collaboration and decision-making process.

J. Dalton, *Great Big Agile*, https://doi.org/10.1007/978-1-4842-4206-3_38

Typical Roles

- Team Member

- Scrum Master

- Other Stakeholders as needed

Desired Behaviors

1. Agree on a basic theme for the session.

2. Attendees write topics to be discussed on sticky notes or cards.

3. Establish a personal or temporary Kanban board with "To Do," "Doing," and "Done" columns.

4. Introduce each topic.

5. Vote, and rank, each topic for discussion.

6. Prioritize the ideas by vote, and move the first to the "Doing" column.

7. Set a time for five minutes, and timebox the discussion of each idea.

8. If the timer goes off, the group can vote for an extension for another five minutes.

9. When time runs out, and no one wishes to continue, move the idea to the "Done" column.

10. Record outcomes and decisions, and distribute to the relevant stakeholders.

CHAPTER 39

Mob Programming

Description

Mob programming is a technique used by a collaborative software development team to rapidly solve a problem, or to write complex software. Mob programming is similar to pair programming, but with two distinctions. First, mob programming uses as many developers as possible so that many perspectives lead to a more complete solution. Secondly, mob programming is performed on-demand, and it is not a standard behavior for the team.

© Jeff Dalton 2019
J. Dalton, *Great Big Agile*, https://doi.org/10.1007/978-1-4842-4206-3_39

Typical Roles

- Agile Team
- Product Owner
- Scrum Master

Desired Behaviors

1. Determine when and how the agile team should use mob programming. Include the conditions and procedures in the agile team's charter or team agreement.

2. Identify the best mix of team members based on the problem to be solved by mob programming.

3. Have the scrum master facilitate the session to make sure it is effective and valuable.

4. Ensure that agile values are exhibited.

5. Ensure that team agreements are respected.

6. Conduct a short retrospective at the end of each session to improve future sessions.

7. Share learning beyond the agile team.

CHAPTER 40

Obeya Room

Description

Obeya is Japanese for "big room." It refers to a dedicated space where team members meet to collaborate and solve problems. It is set in an environment that supports the free flow of information and communication between team members and other stakeholders. An Obeya Room helps to minimize barriers that can stifle communication and inhibit collaboration; and the use of charts, graphs, boards, sticky notes, and other visual information management tools are commonplace in Obeya Rooms as they assist with collaborative problem solving.

J. Dalton, *Great Big Agile*, https://doi.org/10.1007/978-1-4842-4206-3_40

Typical Roles

- Agile Leader
- Agile Team

Desired Behaviors

1. Create a dedicated collaboration area that exists solely to serve as an Obeya room.

2. Assign a defined purpose for each Obeya Room.

3. Ensure that all information is displayed using visual formats (e.g., charts, graphs, dashboards) to communicate information.

CHAPTER 41

Open Space Technology

Description

Open Space Technology is a way to enable a diverse group of people, in any kind of organization, to create inspired meetings and events where the outcome is unclear. In Open Space sessions, participants create and manage their own agenda of parallel working sessions around a central theme of strategic importance.

Open Space works best when the work to be done is complex, the people and ideas involved are diverse, the passion for resolution (and potential for conflict) are high, and there is an urgency to identify solutions.

© Jeff Dalton 2019
J. Dalton, *Great Big Agile*, https://doi.org/10.1007/978-1-4842-4206-3_41

Typical Roles

- Agile Team

- Agile Leader

- Business SME

- Product Owner

Desired Behaviors

1. Identify the major themes that will set the boundaries around Open Space discussions and agendas.

2. Raise issues that are most important to a representative subset of Open Space meeting participants.

3. Plan the Open Space meeting with the assumption that all of the issues and ideas raised will be addressed by those participants most interested, qualified, and capable of resolving them.

4. Conduct the Open Space meeting in a timeframe no longer than one or two days. Within that time, all of the most important ideas, discussion, data, recommendations, conclusions, questions for further study, and plans for immediate action will be documented in one comprehensive report. This report will be finished and in the hands of participants when they leave.

5. Take advantage of visual information techniques, including photographs, to record Open Space information.

6. Prioritize the information generated during the Open Space. This may be done at the end of the Open Space meeting, or in a brief follow-up session.

7. Make the results of the Open Space event available to the entire organization or community within days of the event.

CHAPTER 42

Pair Programming

Description

Pair programming is a software development technique in which two developers work together to complete a coding task. They generally work at one workstation with one programmer being the "driver" and the other being the "navigator." The navigator reviews code as the driver is entering it, performing a sort of real-time code review. While this typically appears increases the cost of programing, the reward of increased code quality far exceeds the investment in time and effort.

Another approach to pair programming has one developer coding, while the other unit tests. In other cases, a developer codes while another sits next to the developer, helping to interpret the requirements and ensuring a higher level of code quality. Regardless of how the pairing is done, the direct and immediate feedback loop of working together improves the quality of the resulting system at a lower cost.

J. Dalton, *Great Big Agile*, https://doi.org/10.1007/978-1-4842-4206-3_42

Typical Roles

1. Software Developers

2. Agile Team

Desired Behaviors

1. Create a physical infrastructure that supports a pair programming working arrangement.

2. Decide the role each developer is going to play, and codify it in the team agreement.

3. Begin pairing and maintain the roles agreed to at the beginning of the pairing session.

4. If at any time during the pairing session, the pair becomes ineffective, revisit the objectives for the session and adjust responsibilities to ensure that the objectives are met.

CHAPTER 43

Peer Reviews

Description

The purpose of a peer review is to ensure that the highest quality is achieved, given the allotted timebox, prior to releasing a work product to the next stage in the process, or to the customer.

© Jeff Dalton 2019
J. Dalton, *Great Big Agile*, https://doi.org/10.1007/978-1-4842-4206-3_43

Typical Roles

- Author

- Agile

- Product Owner (if stories are being reviewed)

- Scrum Master

Desired Behaviors

1. Identify work product for peer review.

2. Identify peer review participants.

3. Distribute content to be reviewed.

4. Confirm review of work products.

5. Conduct peer review with invited reviewers.

6. Record defects, issues, and risks.

7. Add defects and issues to the backlog with assignment to a specific team member.

CHAPTER 44

Planning Poker

Description

Planning Poker is an agile estimation technique that establishes relative sizing using story points and playing cards.

Planning Poker solves the estimation problem by using an estimating game to size backlog items relative to one another. The relative size of a backlog item is intentionally disconnected from the effort in hours to encourage the team to think in a different way: "roughly right" versus "accurately wrong" is the goal.

In Planning Poker, the agile team, working with a scrum master and the product owner, sizes each epic or user story as part of product backlog development or sprint planning. The product owner's role is typically informational only, as they are not involved in building of the actual product.

© Jeff Dalton 2019
J. Dalton, *Great Big Agile*, https://doi.org/10.1007/978-1-4842-4206-3_44

Typical Roles

- Agile Team

- Scrum Master

- Product Owner

Desired Behaviors

1. Review sprint or iteration backlog with the product owner.

2. For each story that has been presented by the product owner, discuss among the team to ensure that an understanding is reached.

3. The scrum master counts down from three, and team members each throw down a card that represents the number of points they believe that story to be.

4. The scrum master facilitates a discussion about why there are differences, ensuring each team member has a chance to present their point of view.

5. The team throws down another set of cards, based on the information they have just received from their teammates.

6. The scrum master facilitates a second round of discussions.

7. If a general consensus is not achieved, discussion continues, and one more round can be played.

8. At the end of three rounds, teams may choose to average the results of the third round, or continue playing until a general consensus is reached.

CHAPTER 45

Product Backlogs

Description

The product backlog is a prioritized list of everything that *may* be included in the product. It can include epics, stories, features, bugs (if the product is in production, or if there have been releases of the product in prior sprints), documentation changes, and any other tasks required by the product owner or agile team. The product owner owns the backlog and the priority of the items on it. The product owner may seek input from stakeholders, business representatives, and the agile team to help set the priority, but the owner is responsible. The backlog is maintained during the sprints through the backlog grooming ceremony.

Additional backlogs may be maintained to prioritize work associated with the team or organization such as the following:

- Impediment Backlog

- Use an impediment backlog to rapidly capture impediments raised during daily stand-ups, keep them visible to the team, and keep progress toward removing them transparent. An impediment is any item that is hindering the work of the team and reducing the likelihood of meeting a commitment.

- Training Backlog

- A training backlog is a prioritized list of training required for the product or organization.

- Improvement Backlog

- An improvement backlog is a prioritized list of improvements for the product or organization.

- Enterprise Impediment Backlog

J. Dalton, *Great Big Agile*, https://doi.org/10.1007/978-1-4842-4206-3_45

- Enterprise impediment backlogs are used to prioritize and manage impediments that are barriers to sustained agile effectiveness and delivering increased value to customers.

- Enterprise Cascading Backlogs

- Enterprise cascading backlogs consist of multiple related backlogs associated with a particular program or organization. These backlogs are managed by a single product owner or product owner team. Managing multiple enterprise cascading backlogs requires a regular pattern and integrated set of practices on a hierarchy of backlogs that facilitates transparency and traceability.

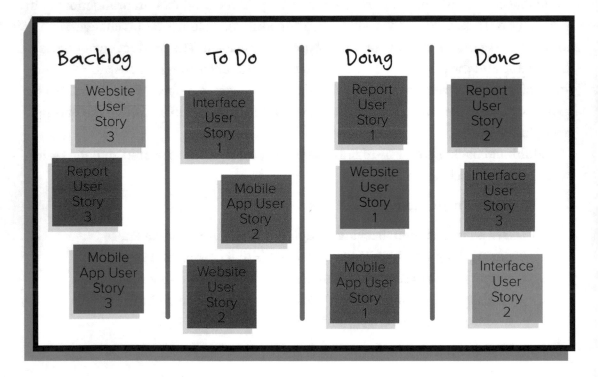

Typical Roles

- Agile Team
- Scrum Master
- Product Owner

Desired Behaviors

1. Ensure that all backlogs are a set of prioritized features, both functional and nonfunctional, which are known to be needed, and are the single, authoritative sources of needs for the product or service.

2. Ensure the backlog is owned by a product owner, and that they are responsible for prioritizing and managing it through the use of the backlog grooming ceremony.

3. Keep the backlog as the foundation of an agile project regardless of the ceremonies and techniques being employed.

4. Make the backlog available to all team members using visual information management techniques.

CHAPTER 46

Product Scenarios

Description

Product scenarios are used to describe how a user will interact with a product to perform actions to achieve a specified goal and tie the who, what, when, why, where, and how in order to provide the overall context of those user actions. In order for a product scenario to be effective, it utilizes user profiles (personas) and focuses on the key interactions between the user and the product. The use of product scenarios can help narrow the focus to which product features would provide the most value to customers.

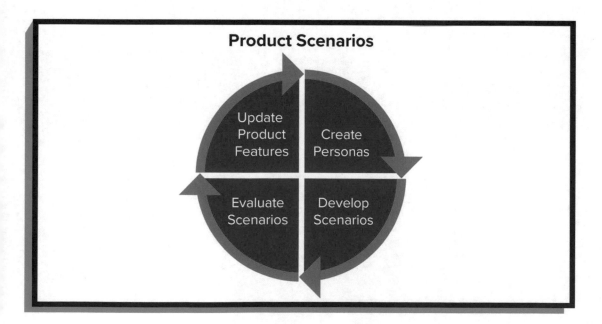

© Jeff Dalton 2019
J. Dalton, *Great Big Agile*, https://doi.org/10.1007/978-1-4842-4206-3_46

Typical Roles

- Agile Team

- Product Management Team

- Business SMEs

- Product Owner

Desired Behaviors

1. Adopt user profiles or personas in product scenarios.

2. Focus on the actions that end users perform in pursuit of a goal.

3. Scenarios should be technology and system agnostic.

CHAPTER 47

Project (Team) Chartering

Description

The Project (Team) Charter summarizes the project or team's objectives, scope boundaries, behaviors, and cultural characteristics. The team collaborates to develop the Project (Team) Charter in order to define the common purpose they are working toward. Topics to be considered for inclusion are:

- Agile Values

- Common expectations

- Communications

- Agreements between the team and suppliers

- Agreements between the team and internal service providers

- Governance and self-organization guidelines

- Roles and Accountabilities

© Jeff Dalton 2019
J. Dalton, *Great Big Agile*, https://doi.org/10.1007/978-1-4842-4206-3_47

Typical Roles

- Agile Team
- Scrum Master

Desired Behaviors

1. Identify high-priority agile values or other organizational guidelines to adopted.

2. Hold a dedicated session to agree on mission, purpose, core values, potential obstacles, ground rules, and communications.

3. Capture information during this session to ensure that the source of the project charter is available to all team members.

4. Ensure that the project (team) charter is understood and subscribed to by all members of a team.

5. Post the charter in a visible location.

6. Plan how often the charter will be reviewed and updated after it has been established.

CHAPTER 48

Prototyping/Spike

Description

A prototype, or sometimes called a "spike" if it's limited in scope or functionality, is a technique used by agile teams to create a product or service proof-of-concept in order to quickly solicit feedback about the design from customers and end users, or to help the team understand the user stories (see "Spike (Design Spike) for more information). Prototypes or spikes can be developed in various ways depending on the type of feedback desired. For example, they can be created using basic materials (e.g., pen and paper) or sophisticated technologies (e.g., markup languages). Prototypes or spikes allow customers to interact with a product giving product teams insight into which features are most important to the end user. The ability to experiment with multiple prototype iterations, and test various concepts in the field, provides critical input into refining the product vision.

J. Dalton, *Great Big Agile*, https://doi.org/10.1007/978-1-4842-4206-3_48

Typical Roles

- Product Owner

- Product Management Team

- Agile Team

- End Users

Desired Behaviors

1. Design prototypes/spikes to generate feedback on features, characteristics, and usability.

2. Observe end users as they explore each prototype/spike.

3. Gather end-user information to help refine the overall product direction.

4. Experiment with multiple iterations of prototypes/spikes.

5. Groom the product backlog after each prototype/spike to ensure that specific functionality is added, removed, or updated.

CHAPTER 49

Release Planning

Description

The purpose of release planning is to project a long-term plan for delivering specific functionality on a loose schedule to meet a business requirement. The used of fixed plans, budget, and functionality, commonly seen in "waterfall-style" planning, is discouraged. The release plan is vision, based on known variables, of what may be released along a given timeline.

Release Planning requires a prioritized product backlog that is managed by the product owner, and is a view into the *potential* functionality that might exist at a specific point in time. The product owner is responsible for conveying the product vision and business objectives to the development team, and discussing a basic sequence of iterations or sprints that, if nothing changes, would result in a delivery schedule. During release planning, the product owner and the agile team collaborate on which features will be delivered in each release, and the agile team can plan for needed capabilities and resources, sprint duration, and estimate the expected number of sprints that may be required to meet the release forecast.

The product owner, in collaboration with the agile teams, should review and revise the release plan after each iteration or sprint, based on feedback received during sprint demos and backlog grooming.

© Jeff Dalton 2019
J. Dalton, *Great Big Agile*, https://doi.org/10.1007/978-1-4842-4206-3_49

Typical Roles

- Agile Team

- Customer

- Business SME

- Marketing, Sales, or Business Development

- Product Owner

Desired Behaviors

1. Prioritize the product backlog and product features during and after each iteration/sprint.

2. Focus on the highest-value features in the early sprints, leaving the lower-value features until later sprints, or even negotiate them away after the teams learn more about them.

3. Loosely allocate epics or stories to sprints within the release plan based on their known variables and business priority.

CHAPTER 50

Retrospectives

Description

The purpose of a retrospective is for each team or functional group to reflect on actions, results, and behaviors from the current sprint, and identify potential improvements for the next. Retrospectives align to one of the core principals from the Agile Manifesto, which states "at regular intervals, the team reflects on how to become more effective, then tunes and adjusts its behavior accordingly."

Retrospectives should be conducted regularly at the conclusion of each iteration or sprint to capture feedback and encourage continuous improvement. There are many different types of retrospectives, but they are all similar in purpose: to learn and improve.

During a retrospective, a team or functional group identifies what went well, what did not go well, and then identifies what actions might be taken to improve performance during the next iteration or sprint. An effective retrospective requires that each participant feels comfortable providing feedback, and it is important that the scrum master/facilitator works to build trust collaborative relationships among team members.

© Jeff Dalton 2019
J. Dalton, *Great Big Agile*, https://doi.org/10.1007/978-1-4842-4206-3_50

Enterprise Retrospective

The intention of an Enterprise Retrospective is to improve the performance of an overall organization. This retrospective is not just one agile team, but multiple, often represented by each scrum master. This ceremony should be planned out to identify the schedule, approach, location, and process scope. This retrospective may have a reduced frequency as it is more resource intensive than a Team Retrospective, and may not be aligned with a specific sprint.

Heartbeat Retrospective

A Heartbeat Retrospective begins with ensuring the team is fully aware that the purpose is to learn from mistakes and not assign blame. Other characteristics of this type of retrospective includes a timeboxed approach with a maximum of 90 minutes, taking place outside the normal team room, and the team deciding who is welcome to attend this meeting.

Sprint Retrospective

While all agile teams should work to continuously improve, it is important to set aside time to proactively find ways to improve. The Sprint Retrospective is conducted at the end of each sprint, and the entire team, including the scrum master and product owner (if there is a high level of trust) should participate. Typically, a Sprint Retrospective is one hour, but may vary based on how long the spring duration was and whether there are contentious topics to discuss.

Training Retrospective

The purpose of a Training Retrospective is to periodically review how well training is working for a team, functional group, or organization. This retrospective should include all relevant stakeholders such as agile leaders, team members, trainers, mentors, and coaches.

Milestone Retrospective

For a project or initiative that has been underway for an extended duration, or has been completed, a Milestone Retrospective can be valuable. This retrospective takes more time because of the length of the project being reviewed, and could span for one to three days. Milestone retrospectives are generally facilitated by someone external to the team to review long-term or strategic impacts, work relationships, and governance.

Confirmation Retrospective

A Confirmation Retrospective is intended to review training results in order to improve an overall organization. This retrospective may allow teams to practice new skills or training methods to solidify training approaches and ensure that there is consistency across the organization.

Typical Roles

- Agile Team

- Functional Group

- Scrum Master

Desired Behaviors

1. Establish a regular frequency for retrospectives.

2. Gather team or functional group to conduct retrospective at the end of each sprint or iteration, if appropriate.

3. During each retrospective, discuss challenges and capture lessons learned.

4. During retrospective, discuss and capture what went well, what did not go well, and ideas for improvement for the next sprint.

5. At the conclusion of the retrospective, identify actions to be taken to improve.

6. Add actionable items to the improvement backlog.

CHAPTER 51

Review

Description

Review is a well-defined and formal method for ensuring that a work product meets team or organizational expectations, and to ensure that defects are identified and corrected as early as possible. Review is an opportunity to "fail fast." Unlike a Gemba Walk, which is to "go and see," a review is to "ask, record, and provide feedback." Reviews are useful to gather a broad set of perspectives, develop knowledge of less-experienced team members, and to standardize improvements across teams and the organization. Reviews can be informal observations, or can use formal checklists and process baselines, but should always generate data that can be used to share learning and prevent the recurrence of common problems.

© Jeff Dalton 2019
J. Dalton, *Great Big Agile*, https://doi.org/10.1007/978-1-4842-4206-3_51

Typical Roles

- Reviewer

- Scrum Master

- Agile Team

- Functional Group Members

Desired Behaviors

1. Review against a set of common expectations.

2. Ensure that everyone is aware of both the content and timing of a review.

3. Gather useful data and information that can improve the team, group, or organization.

4. Have an objective team member facilitate the review.

5. Add improvements and impediments discovered during reviews to the appropriate backlogs.

CHAPTER 52

Roles and Accountabilities Game

Description

The purpose of the "Roles and Accountabilities" game is to build a common understanding of team roles and accountabilities, and to encourage self-subscription to accountabilities. This game identifies key roles and accountabilities on index cards, then has the team align the accountabilities to each role. While aligning accountabilities, the team can work through ambiguous or contentious accountabilities, and the scrum master may assist by helping team members reach the best conclusion. This game may be applied to different types of teams in an organization where clarity and common understanding are needed. At the conclusion of the game, team members can self-subscribe to roles, and all the accountabilities for each role that have been defined.

© Jeff Dalton 2019
J. Dalton, *Great Big Agile*, https://doi.org/10.1007/978-1-4842-4206-3_52

Typical Roles

- Agile Team

- Functional Team

- Scrum Master

Desired Behaviors

1. Identify participants that are needed for the roles and accountabilities game.

2. Prepare for the game. Provide large sticky notes for roles, small sticky notes for accountabilities, wall space, and markers.

3. Divide the participants into groups, with two groups being sufficient for smaller teams.

4. Using a timeboxed approach, ask each team to define all potential roles within the team, and post them on large sticky notes.

5. Each group peer reviews the other's work, and adds/removes/combines roles as appropriate.

6. Each team discusses and defines the accountabilities for each role and records them under the appropriate roles.

7. Each group peer reviews the other's work, and adds/removes/combines accountabilities as appropriate.

8. Team members can now self-subscribe to roles that have been defined.

CHAPTER 53

Scrum of Scrums

Description

Scrum of Scrums is a technique that enables the effective synchronization among interrelated teams. Each team designates a representative, often the scrum master, to participate in the scrum of scrums events, and to ensure that the teams are coordinated and synchronized. The scrum of scrums encourages a daily meeting where the representatives communicate and collaborate about issues, risks, and status across teams.

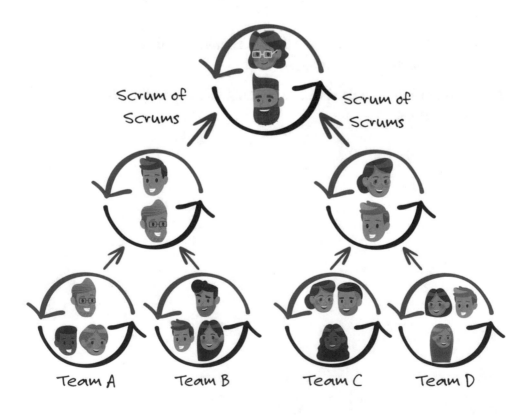

© Jeff Dalton 2019
J. Dalton, *Great Big Agile*, https://doi.org/10.1007/978-1-4842-4206-3_53

Typical Roles

- Agile Leader

- Scrum of Scrums Master

- Team Representative (often the scrum master from each team)

Desired Behaviors

1. Each scrum team identifies a representative to share information at the scrum of scrums events.

2. The scrum of scrums meeting should occur daily at the same time.

3. Each representative should share what was completed by their team, next steps, and impediments from the team they are representing.

4. Discussions will focus on coordination between teams and clarify responsibilities and boundaries.

5. An independent backlog will be maintained for the scrum of scrums team.

CHAPTER 54

Scrum Wall/Scrum Board

A scrum wall/scrum board is a visual information radiator for displaying the current state of user stories and tasks within a team. Transparency is an important principle in scrum, and the scrum board is a way for a project to display what is being worked on, what is in progress, and what has been completed. If the team is at one location, then a physical scrum board is recommended, but distributed teams may wish to implement tools within popular agile application life-cycle management systems. The scrum board is continuously updated throughout each sprint.

© Jeff Dalton 2019
J. Dalton, *Great Big Agile*, https://doi.org/10.1007/978-1-4842-4206-3_54

Typical Roles

- Agile Team
- Scrum Master

Desired Behaviors

1. Identify a location for the scrum board. Ideally this is in a place that the team will be able to view it throughout the day.

2. Prepare a wall surface and gather needed supplies such as markers, sticky notes, and tape. Alternatively, magnetic cards can be used with aluminum white boards.

3. Identify the columns for the items that will be tracked. The columns that are generally used are:

   a. Sprint backlog.

   b. To do: Place for all cards that are not in the "Done" or "In Process" columns for the current sprint.

   c. Work in process (WIP): Any card currently being worked on goes in the WIP or "doing" column. Each team member self-subscribes to a story, and moves it to the WIP column when ready to start work on the story.

   d. Verify: Many tasks have corresponding test tasks stories. These are placed in the "verify" column.

   e. Done: Completed cards are moved to the "done" column and are removed at the end of the sprint.

4. Create a card for each user story in the current sprint.

5. Create a card for each task in the current sprint.

6. At any time, team members can update task information.

7. During the daily stand-up, the board should be updated by moving cards to the appropriate columns if required.

CHAPTER 55

Self-Selection/ Self-Subscription

Description

Self-Selection/Self-Subscription is a core agile value that encourages team members to own their decisions by selecting the work that they will do based on skills, interest, and the team's needs. It works best when used during a facilitated ceremony where a scrum master or another facilitator ensures that product owners, project managers, other managers, or other outside influences are not tasking individual team members. The highest level of team member commitment is achieved via self-selection, a technique that enables self-organization.

J. Dalton, *Great Big Agile*, https://doi.org/10.1007/978-1-4842-4206-3_55

Typical Roles

- Agile Team
- Product Owner
- Scrum Master

Desired Behaviors

1. Encourage self-selection as a core value in the organization.

2. Incorporate self-selection in all planning ceremonies where work is connected to the team members who will complete it.

3. Scrum masters should ensure that all stakeholders respect self-selection and to coach those who do not.

CHAPTER 56

Spike (Design Spike)

Description

A Spike is a solution-specific experiment, often taking place during an entire sprint, but sometimes in shorter durations, aimed at answering a question or gathering information important to the team's success.

Spikes are sometimes referred to as "design spikes," or "sprint prototypes," and are described as the simplest output (typically code, but often a design or other work product) that can be built to confirm the team is on the right track.

Teams will often routinely include stories for experimentation with spikes during sprints early in the produce development life cycle.

© Jeff Dalton 2019
J. Dalton, *Great Big Agile*, https://doi.org/10.1007/978-1-4842-4206-3_56

Typical Roles

- Team Members
- Scrum Master

Desired Behaviors

1. Develop a user story for spikes as if they were any other backlog item.

2. Estimate using story points, or hours if they are at the task level.

3. Develop tasks, if required.

4. Demonstrate outcomes internally to team members.

5. Gather data for input into backlog grooming.

CHAPTER 57

Sprint

Description

A sprint is a timeboxed event where most work gets done, and typically has a duration of two to four weeks. Several ceremonies are embedded in a typical sprint, including sprint planning, sprint demos/reviews, retrospectives, daily stand-ups, and backlog grooming.

A sprint should begin with sprint planning and end with a retrospective. Some agile teams allocate days prior and after each sprint to conduct planning and retrospectives, but the outcome is more predictable to include it within the sprint.

During a project, sprints should have a consistent duration. When one sprint ends, another immediately begins. Each sprint should have a defined goal, and no changes in scope should be made during a sprint. At the end of each sprint, a set of user stories should be completed and ready to deliver to the customer, although it is common to put completed code "on the shelf" waiting for other interdependent stories to be completed.

Sprints may be used for other purposes, including:

- An envisioning sprint is for developing a long-term product vision.

- A *sprint zero* sets up the basic infrastructure for a project.

- A *design sprint* is for developing a high-level design.

- An *improvement sprint* is for developing and deploying performance improvements.

© Jeff Dalton 2019
J. Dalton, *Great Big Agile*, https://doi.org/10.1007/978-1-4842-4206-3_57

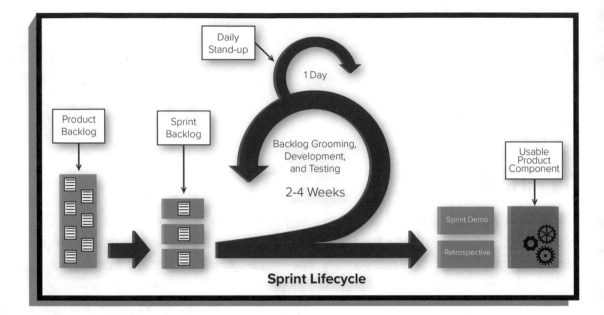

Typical Roles

- Agile Team
- Agile Leader
- Scrum Master
- Product Owner
- Process Improvement Team Members (for improvement sprints)

Desired Behaviors

1. Establish key roles such as product owner, scrum master, and team members.

2. Determine sprint duration.

3. Identify the ceremonies that the agile team will use during each sprint. Define the day, time, and duration for each ceremony.

4. Conduct sprint planning to create the sprint backlog, and have each agile team member select the user stories for which they will be accountable.

5. Conduct daily stand-ups to understand progress, impediments, and risks.

6. Conduct backlog grooming to maintain the backlogs and develop a view for the next sprint.

7. Complete user stories in the sprint backlog.

8. Conduct a sprint demo/review to demonstrate what was completed during the sprint.

9. Conduct a sprint retrospective to learn what went well, what did not go well, and action items for improvement during the next sprint.

10. Repeat sprints until the product backlog has been depleted, funding runs out, or until the project ends.

CHAPTER 58

Sprint Demo

Description

A Sprint Demo (also called Sprint Review or Show and Tell) is a collaborative technique used to ensure that key stakeholders are aware of, and accept, the value being delivered at the end of each sprint. During the sprint demo, the work that was completed, as well as the forecasted work that was not completed, is demonstrated to the product owner and other customers.

The sprint demo occurs at the end of each sprint, immediately prior to the retrospective; and is a form of acceptance, communication, validation, and recognition that the team has reached its intended goal.

© Jeff Dalton 2019
J. Dalton, *Great Big Agile*, https://doi.org/10.1007/978-1-4842-4206-3_58

Typical Roles

- Agile Team

- Customer

- Product Owner

- Scrum Master

Desired Behaviors

1. The work completed for each user story delivered in the sprint is compared against the criteria described in the definition of done.

2. The project stakeholders participate to ensure that expectations were met, and any issues are addressed. An explanation may resolve an issue, or an adjustment might need to be made to the product backlog.

3. Proper planning of the sprint demo is required in order to ensure that the correct stakeholders are present, the right technology is installed, and that the agenda is set and agreed to. The goals of the sprint demo should be distributed in advance.

4. The sprint demo should be integrated into the milestones of the top-level plan.

5. Any issues with the attendance of key stakeholders should be identified and addressed immediately to minimize disruptions.

6. The team should address any questions about the work accomplished during the sprint during the meeting. Issues that cannot be resolved should result in new backlog stories or updates to existing stories.

CHAPTER 59

Sprint Planning

Description

A sprint planning meeting occurs at the beginning of each sprint, and is a negotiation between the agile team and the product owner as to what value can be delivered in the upcoming sprint. During the sprint planning meeting, a sprint backlog is developed and tasks are identified to support the forecasted user stories. Team members assess how much work they can accomplish during the sprint based on known velocity, and the team members subscribe to the various stories and tasks to be completed.

A sprint planning meeting should take place at the beginning of each sprint, and should identify the value to be delivered during that sprint. The product backlog, which has already been sized and prioritized, is the primary source of stories for the sprint planning meeting. The goal of sprint planning is to agree on a sprint backlog that aligns with the team's historical velocity and contains tasks, usually estimated in hours, and owners for each story.

A sprint plan that is understood, realistic, and created by the team members who are the same people doing the work is a critical influencer of project success.

© Jeff Dalton 2019
J. Dalton, *Great Big Agile*, https://doi.org/10.1007/978-1-4842-4206-3_59

Typical Roles

- Agile Team

- Product Owner (for context)

- Scrum Master

Desired Behaviors

1. Ensure that the scope of the sprint is clear, and that all work items are included. Teams can easily overlook non-software work products in their planning, including testing and documentation, as these oversights have the potential to negatively affect velocity.

2. Ensure that estimates are provided for all work to be completed during the sprint.

3. Use planning poker, or other relative sizing method, to estimate stories taking care to not to exceed the known velocity.

4. Allow each team member to review the plans and estimates for the sprint prior to committing to the forecast.

5. Set the expectation that adjustments will be made to the sprint plan based on vacations, training, or other external influences that could impact the velocity.

6. Set the expectation that adjustments will be made to the sprint plan based on the team's capability, issues, and risks.

7. Ensure that each team member commits to the plan prior to beginning the sprint.

CHAPTER 60

Stakeholder Identification and Management

Description

Stakeholder identification and management is the process used to identify all stakeholders for a project, and how they will be involved. It is important to understand that not all stakeholders will have the same influence or effect on a project, nor will they be affected in the same manner.

Once stakeholders are identified, a definition of how they interact should be defined by identifying which stakeholders are required at each ceremony, event or milestone. It is helpful to identify expected roles, responsibilities, and frequency of engagement.

An outcome of identifying stakeholders should be a project stakeholder list, matrix, set of sticky notes on a board, or a RASIC (Responsible, Approves, Supports, Informed, Consulted) chart, where attributes such as the level of influence, frequency, and accountabilities are captured.

© Jeff Dalton 2019
J. Dalton, *Great Big Agile*, https://doi.org/10.1007/978-1-4842-4206-3_60

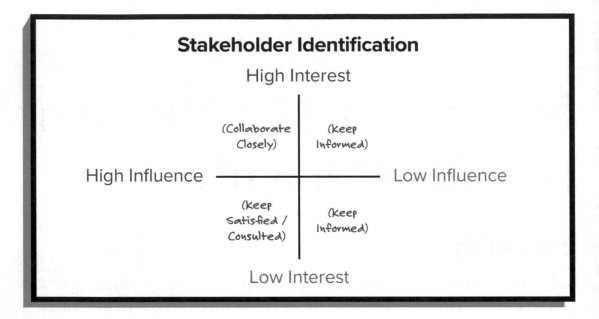

Typical Roles

- Agile Leader
- Agile Team
- Product Owner
- Scrum Master

Desired Behaviors

1. Ensure that stakeholder identification considers project, team, functional groups, and organizational participants.

2. Capture the names, contact information, titles, organizations, and other pertinent information of all stakeholders.

3. After analysis is complete, the level of stakeholder engagement should be estimated and should identify when the stakeholders will participate in project activities.

4. Stakeholder engagement is monitored during the project, and a team engagement score (TeamScore) should be created and trended.

CHAPTER 61

State of the Team

Description

A State of the Team is a gathering of multiple teams to understand what has been accomplished by each team, and what is needed from other teams, functional groups, or leadership. The state of the team allows all stakeholders to understand a global view of all status and progress. This allows leadership to assess the organizational risk profile, and determine where support is needed, as well as an opportunity for teams to learn what others are experiencing. It is an important tool to build trust and understand progress at an organizational level.

Typical Roles

- Agile Leader

- Agile Team

- Product Owner

- Scrum Master

Desired Behaviors

1. Create a schedule of State of the Team meetings.

2. Develop a simple agenda that is common for all team. Teams should not have to prepare, but should be able to summarize information they are already collecting from daily stand-ups, retrospectives, and sprint demos.

3. Go beyond status and capture the best ways to solve each team's problems with the collective experience in the room.

4. Stay agile. The meeting time will depend on the number of teams; however, a good rule of thumb is 15 minutes per team.

CHAPTER 62

SWOT Analysis (Strengths, Weaknesses, Opportunities, Threats)

Description

A SWOT analysis is a strategic planning tool that helps a business entity identify their strengths and weaknesses, as well as opportunities and threats that may exist in a specific business situation. A SWOT analysis is most commonly used as part of a sales or marketing plan, but it is also a good tool for agile teams to use as a starting point for projects or sprints.

A SWOT analysis is usually depicted as a square divided into four quadrants. Each quadrant represents one element of the SWOT analysis (Strengths, Weaknesses, Opportunities, and Threats).

© Jeff Dalton 2019
J. Dalton, *Great Big Agile*, https://doi.org/10.1007/978-1-4842-4206-3_62

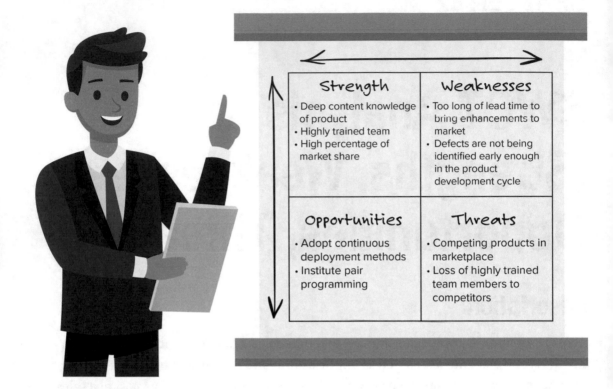

Typical Roles

- Product Owner

- Stakeholders

- Agile Team

- Scrum Master

Desired Behaviors

1. A series of questions are used to begin filling in each quadrant. Start with strengths:

    a. What do we do well?

    b. What are our unique skills?

    c. What expert or specialized knowledge do we have?

    d. What experience do we have?

    e. What do we do better than our competitors?

    f. Where are we most profitable in our business?

2. Weaknesses may include attributes that will impede progress in achieving objectives. Ask questions, such as:

    a. In what areas do we need to improve?

    b. What resources do we lack?

    c. What parts of our business are not as profitable?

    d. Where do we need further education and/or experience?

    e. What costs us time and/or money?

3. Opportunities are external conditions that will help you achieve your objective. Ask questions, such as:

    a. What are the business goals we are currently working toward?

    b. How can we do more with existing customers or clients?

    c. How can we use technology to enhance our business?

    d. Are there new target audiences that we have the potential to reach?

    e. Are there related products and services that provide an opportunity for new business?

4. Threats are external conditions that could damage your business's performance. Ask questions, such as:

    a. What obstacles do we face?

    b. What are the strengths of our biggest competitors?

    c. What are our competitors doing that we are not?

    d. What is going on in the economy?

    e. What is going on in the industry?

5. Follow up on the SWOT analysis:

    a. Create a plan to build strengths.

    b. List ways to work on mitigating weaknesses.

    c. Create a plan to use strengths to eliminate the threats.

    d. Combine strengths and opportunities to develop new strategies.

    e. Review weaknesses and opportunities to create improvement ideas.

CHAPTER 63

Team Agreement

Description

A team agreement is a social contract entered into by members of an agile team to define team behaviors, expectations, and standards. Some team agreements are simple ideas written on a white board, while others are detailed charters that contain important facts about the team itself. Team agreements are typically developed at the beginning of a release and can be updated after each sprint retrospective or sprint demo.

Self-organization is an important goal for any agile team, and a self-organized team clearly defines the parameters for team operations. Individual agile team members may have specialized skills and areas of focus, but accountability belongs to the team as a whole. A simple yet compelling team vision is an excellent way to get upper-level management behind a project.

© Jeff Dalton 2019
J. Dalton, *Great Big Agile*, https://doi.org/10.1007/978-1-4842-4206-3_63

Typical Roles

- Agile Team
- Scrum Master

Desired Behaviors

1. Create a shared vision that helps the team have an identity and a common purpose. A shared vision should be visible, compelling, and understandable by any stakeholder who sees it.

2. Make sure the resources needed by the team to achieve the shared vision are available.

3. Select a name for your team and record it in the team agreement.

4. Set the expectation that the shared vision is a living document that should be updated and improved as the team learns through the product development process.

CHAPTER 64

Team Estimation Game

Description

The Team Estimating Game (sometimes called the Fibonacci Team Estimating Game) is an agile estimation technique that establishes relative sizing using story points and a rough order of magnitude estimation. Planning Poker is a similar technique that uses playing cards to depict story points.

This agile technique tries to solve the estimation problem by using an estimating game to size backlog items relative to one another. The relative size of a backlog item is intentionally disconnected from effort in hours to encourage the team to think in a different way. "Roughly right" versus "accurately wrong" is the ultimate goal of the team estimation game.

The scrum team, working with a scrum master and product owner, sizes each epic or user story as part of product backlog grooming or sprint planning. The product owner's role is typically informational only, as they are not involved in the building of the actual product.

© Jeff Dalton 2019
J. Dalton, *Great Big Agile*, https://doi.org/10.1007/978-1-4842-4206-3_64

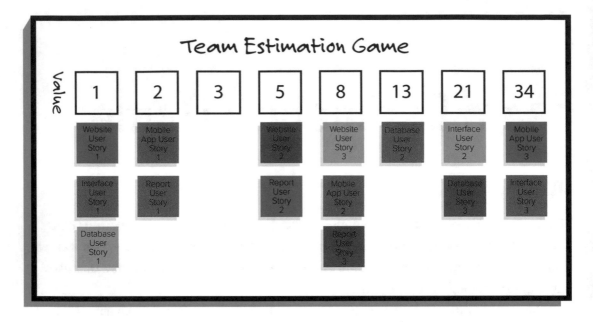

Typical Roles

- Agile Team
- Product Owner
- Scrum Master

Desired Behaviors

1. Use cards or sticky notes with user stories that are placed on a board.

2. The game consists of three rounds of collaborative sizing negotiation by the agile team.

3. To begin the game, a single story is pulled off the backlog and placed in the middle of the board.

4. During each round, stories are taken off the backlog and placed on the board in a location that is either larger (to the right) or smaller (to the left) than the stories that are already on the board. Each team member is allowed to change the location of one of story, as long as they can logically explain the reason for the change. They may choose to either place a new story, or move an existing story, but not both.

5. After each round, the team discusses the sequence of stories on the board, with each team member offering advice based on their area of expertise.

6. Once relative sizing is determined, numbers in the Fibonacci sequence are drawn on the board, and stories are moved to the left or right under the appropriate number based on the team's understanding of the complexity and risk of the story. The basic order of the stories cannot be changed.

7. Always use the Fibonacci sequence, as this is the recommended unit of measure for relative story-point sizing.

CHAPTER 65

Team Room Set-Up

Description

An agile team should have their own space, known as a Team Room. Team room set-up is typically done when a new team is formed, or a new project is set to begin. Elements of a team room that need to be considered are listed below.

- Location

- Size of the room

- Workstation that supports pair programming

- White Boards/Flip Charts

- Task Boards

- Furniture that supports ad hoc collaboration

See Chapter 10 on **Agile Digs** for more information on an agile team's workspace.

© Jeff Dalton 2019
J. Dalton, *Great Big Agile*, https://doi.org/10.1007/978-1-4842-4206-3_65

Typical Roles

- Agile Leader
- Agile Team
- Scrum Master

Desired Behaviors

1. Secure the dedicated space for each agile team.
2. Identify the room layout and all key elements that will be needed.
3. Purchase or secure all elements for the team room.
4. Assemble the team room and reevaluate assembly during retrospectives.

CHAPTER 66

Technical Debt

Description

Technical Debt is incurred when the agile team proactively determines that a less optimum, less efficient, or less robust solution is appropriate given constraints of time, budget, or resources. As this graphic from Martin Fowler describes, as technical debt increases, the costs and effort to continue development, or maintain an existing system, will become too high, and a "technical debt sprint" should be scheduled within a release to improve code quality.

The challenge for any Development Team is that:

- The business community likes technical debt due to short-term gains.

- The technical community dislikes technical debt due to long-term pain.

Technical Debt Quadrant

	Reckless	Prudent
Deliberate	We don't have time for design.	We must ship now and deal with the consequences.
Accidental	What's layering?	Now we know how we should have done it.

© Jeff Dalton 2019
J. Dalton, *Great Big Agile*, https://doi.org/10.1007/978-1-4842-4206-3_66

Typical Roles

- Agile Team

- Scrum Master

Desired Behaviors

1. Quantify the technical debt and balance the business needs with the technical needs of your projects.

2. Leverage the practices in sprint planning to plan, prioritize, and sequence the elimination of technical debt by allocating them as user stories to future sprints and releases.

3. The decision to incur technical debt should be proactive and not the result of defects or coding errors.

CHAPTER 67

Test-Driven Development

Description

Test-driven development (TDD) is an agile technique where a developer will write a basic test case to verify the desired functionality, knowing that it will fail, and then writes the minimum amount of code to pass the test. The developer will then enhance the code to ensure that it meets acceptable performance and coding standards and principles.

Test-driven development brings the most value when used with short sprints, where rapid experimentation is possible.

J. Dalton, *Great Big Agile*, https://doi.org/10.1007/978-1-4842-4206-3_67

Typical Roles

- Agile Team

Desired Behaviors

1. Incrementally create test cases and related software that fails initially, but eventually passes each test case. An automated test framework is normally used to encourage efficiency.

2. If manual testing is used, save test cases for the future to ensure that changes to the software do not cause unintended defects.

3. Use the test case inventory to evaluate requirements changes.

CHAPTER 68

Three Diverse Humans

Description

Three Diverse Humans, or TDH, is a User Story and Design validation technique that involves review and input for three separate, but equal, individuals prior to Product Backlog generation, or commitment to a complex design. The typical TDH session is a one-hour, rapid fire meeting that includes a developer, an analyst/SME, and a tester, but it can be attended by alternative roles as well.

J. Dalton, *Great Big Agile*, https://doi.org/10.1007/978-1-4842-4206-3_68

Typical Roles

- Developer
- Analyst/SME
- Tester
- Others as Alternates

Desired Behaviors

1. The TDH session begins with an agreement of the backlog stories or design to be reviewed.

2. Five minutes of discussion, led by the author of the work product.

3. Feedback by non-author participants from their perspective. For example, a tester might provide feedback of additional tools, environments, or technology that is required, while a developer may offer suggestions for downsizing a story.

4. The User Story or Design is adjusted in real time, if possible, or placed on the backlog for a design sprint, spike, or backlog grooming session.

CHAPTER 69

Training

Description

Agile teams are learning teams. There are different ways to train team members, but each one should be designed with outcomes that build capability. Organizations should identify what training methods will work best for each scenario, and ensure that all team members have the capabilities to meet their commitments.

- Professional Training is typically related to a certification or a profession.
- Technical Training is related to the technological aspects of the job.
- Soft Skills are communication and personal skills that help to ensure success in the work environment.
- Team Training addresses the process the team agrees to adopt.

© Jeff Dalton 2019
J. Dalton, *Great Big Agile*, https://doi.org/10.1007/978-1-4842-4206-3_69

Typical Roles

- Agile Leader

- Agile Team

- Scrum Master

- Product Owner

- Trainer/Coach

Desired Behaviors

1. Determine organizational and team training needs. This may be captured in a training backlog.

2. Ensure that consideration is given to training goals, budget, and resources.

3. Develop a plan of execution that includes what training method will be used and a timeline.

4. Ensure that accountability is assigned for accomplishing planned training and monitoring to completion.

CHAPTER 70

Unit Testing

Description

Unit testing is a technique applied by individual software developers to ensure that the smallest, self-contained pieces of code function as designed and provide the correct results. Because manual unit testing is time and effort intensive, many tools exist to automatically run unit tests based on design elements coded directly within code modules. Continuous Build/Integration tools ensure that code is unit tested with no failures prior to check-in of code.

© Jeff Dalton 2019
J. Dalton, *Great Big Agile*, https://doi.org/10.1007/978-1-4842-4206-3_70

Typical Roles

- Agile Team

- Organization (e.g., Infrastructure or Support)

Desired Behaviors

1. Provide the infrastructure and support at the organizational level to implement automated unit testing for each team.

2. Create team agreement items related to unit testing all code.

3. Ensure that the developers are trained in how to design code to support automated unit testing.

4. Ensure that automated testing provides demonstrable value, and improves scripts if it does not.

CHAPTER 71

Velocity

Description

Velocity is a historical definition of a given team's ability to deliver value during a consistent sprint duration.

Velocity is used by agile teams for sprint and capacity planning, and to predict whether teams will successfully meet their sprint forecast.

Velocity is team and duration specific, meaning that as a team changes, they cannot expect its velocity (value delivered) to remain constant. Any change to the team or sprint duration will affect the team's ability to deliver.

During sprint planning, an agile team will set a velocity objective for the sprint based on historical data. A burn down (or burn up) is used to depict a team's actual velocity during a sprint or release.

© Jeff Dalton 2019
J. Dalton, *Great Big Agile*, https://doi.org/10.1007/978-1-4842-4206-3_71

Typical Roles

- Agile Team

- Scrum Master

- Product Owner

Desired Behaviors

1. Depend on velocity for sprint planning if the team and duration remain constant.

2. Do not attempt to normalize velocity or story-point values across multiple teams.

3. Do not attempt to assign hours or days to story points. The usefulness of velocity is based on its unit of measure being value, not time.

CHAPTER 72

Visual Information Management

Description

Visual information management is the practice of using information visualization techniques to depict important information to a large group of people. Visual information management is a clear, simple, and effective way to organize and present the result of a team's work. It can also be perceived as fun by the teams, since visual elements bring color and life into an otherwise sterile office environment. Visual management will positively influence the behavior and attitude of team members, managers, and stakeholders by helping build transparency and trust.

The term "information radiator" is used to describe any artifact that conveys project information and is publicly displayed in the workspace. Information radiators are an essential component of visual information management, and they can be any handwritten, drawn, printed, or an electronic display that the team places in a highly visible location.

© Jeff Dalton 2019
J. Dalton, *Great Big Agile*, https://doi.org/10.1007/978-1-4842-4206-3_72

Typical Roles

- Agile Team
- Product Owner
- Scrum Master

Desired Behaviors

1. Use highly visible information radiators to convey cultural norms:

   a. The organization is committed to transparency.

   b. The organization is committed to high trust.

2. Use information radiators elicit conversation when visitors are with the team.

3. Take advantage of white boards, flip charts, poster boards, or large electronic displays as information radiators.

4. Regularly update information radiators to keep the teams interested and informed.

PART IV

Next Steps for Leaders

CHAPTER 73

Using the Agile Performance Holarchy

Successfully transforming an organization where leadership practices traditional command and control, to one that is agile and self-organizing, will bring you numerous benefits, but it's not as simple as adopting a few scrum ceremonies. As powerful as those ceremonies are, they are only part of the picture. During this chapter, I'll describe my own journey to an agile leadership state, along with what worked, what didn't, and what I would do differently next time (sound familiar?).

When I started my first company in 2005, I didn't know much about the formal theories and techniques of agility, although what I learned in my years as a musician and at other companies was a good starting point. Agile was just starting to become popular, and no one was using it for company operations. Although several good books have been written on this subject since then, it wasn't like business schools were teaching something as radical as less power for CEOs! I knew, from my years in professional orchestras and leading software teams, that it was *good,* that people *wanted it,* and I knew that high trust was a *desirable* state – but those things don't get you there – infrastructure is required!. We all want to be agile, but the forces of customers, regulations, accounting, and culture are powerful forces that often work against us. Building and deploying a high-trust, agile, and self-organizing company was just not something that was being done at scale, and there were few examples to guide me. And the business schools in Ann Arbor, Cambridge, or Stanford were never going to turn the tables on their MBA students and admit that what they've been doing for a hundred years was wrong. In fact, some of these institutions, based on the articles they still publish today, *still* don't seem to get it!

My first job in Information Technology was as a Director of Data Processing at St. Mary's College. It was a fancy title for "computer guy," and in 1986, that meant something! I wasn't re-booting Windows or troubleshooting the "Blue Screen of Death"

J. Dalton, *Great Big Agile*, https://doi.org/10.1007/978-1-4842-4206-3_73

for my customers. My days consisted of writing software on an IBM System 36 (you haven't lived until you've coded in RPG!), pulling cable through a series of underground steam tunnels, fleshing out requirements for everything from student records to holiday fundraising cards, and automating the school bookstore. And, my favorite task of all, making donated Data General terminals work with donated IBM green screens. That may not seem like a challenge these days, but back then we didn't have protocol converters to just plug things into, and everything had to be hand coded (by me) in Assembler. Good times!

I still look back on that job as the most lean and agile position I've ever held, and best training I've ever had. Not only did I learn new and interesting things every day, but the nature of the job literally forced me to become an expert at agility, while I collaborated with numerous departments, managers, teachers, and students to make everything work in the leanest environment I've ever been in. In the 1980s few people were computer literate, so I was given complete autonomy to be accountable for "the system," which of course included the *process*, which was way more than just the software and hardware required to run the college. This was a lot of power for a recent college grad, albeit one who was on his second career. None of us worked for the other, but we had to self-organize around the solutions in order to get anything done. The principles I had learned during my decades of music study – trust, transparency collaboration, and the rest, continued to set the tone for the rest of my career.

Following my years at St. Mary's, I joined Electronic Data Systems (EDS), a large systems integrator that built systems for General Motors, where I ended up leading an autonomous team that managed systems in Kuwait, Dubai, Puerto Rico, and throughout Africa and South America. Due to the absence of the internet and cell phones, we were completely independent, and the self-organizing principles I had learned in music, and transferred to St. Mary's, continued to evolve as that team proved to be successful without significant management oversight. I spent more than a few nights stripping cable with my teeth, cursing at 300 bps modems that wouldn't connect from Abu Dhabi, and bribing local x.25 officials with cartons of cigarettes. Our team did whatever it took.

After EDS, I spent five years with Ernst and Young, LLC, where I had an opportunity to work with a team of some of the most talented and innovative people I had ever known. These people were so skilled in the basic principles of agility and self-organization that they required almost zero management from the beginning, and as a leader I learned that it was my job to provide an *infrastructure* for self-organization, not to manage them, and to run interference for the team, protecting them from the command-and-control bureaucrats, and work to inspire them by demonstrating high trust, transparency, and a willingness to serve. Many from that team were with me at two other companies, where I served as Vice President of Global Consulting, and many have since joined us at Broadsword where we continue to evolve our agile business practices as a company.

The Most Important Value Is Trust

Most of us are familiar with the core agile values described in the Agile Manifesto, as well as the seven Agile Team values described in *Exploring Scrum: The Fundamentals, 2nd ed.*, by Dan Rawsthorne and Doug Shimp (CreateSpace Independent Publishing Platform, 2011), and we are reminded of their importance at software conferences, and within a plethora of articles, books and blogs. Trust, transparency, collaboration, fail fast, and the others are seared into the brains of any agilest, but which is the most important? Which is the *Value of all Values*? How does a leader build an environment where values, ceremonies, and techniques are habitual and extend in *everything* we do in a company or agency?

It all starts with trust. If we don't have trust, there is no transformation. If trust is not pervasive, there is no agility, and there is no self-organization. Although the application of agile in business operations is relatively new, the landscape is already littered with failed and ineffective agile deployments where teams did their level best to adopt ceremonies like daily stand-ups, sprint planning, and retrospectives, but their culture became an impediment to success that could not be overcome.

Ceremonies don't make you agile, nor do they enable self-organization. Trust does. Culture does. Leadership does. But, leaders at all levels can't simply declare that an organization is suddenly "high trust." If only it worked that way!

Years ago, when I was a Senior Manager with Ernst and Young, I was waiting in the office of the CTO of one of the "Big Three" auto companies, and the young consultant that was with me pointed to a cartoon on her wall. It went something like this:

Hi, I'm your consultant.

That's a combination of "con" and "insult."

Yes, let me consult you.

"It doesn't seem like he trusts consultants," the young newbie said to me. "That makes me kind of nervous."

"He may feel that way about some consultants," I said, "but let's make sure he never feels that way about us."

"How do we do that? He seems to hate consultants."

"Easy. Pretend he's your neighbor. How would you treat them?"

Looking at the ceiling, he sighed and said, "I try to be credible, meet my commitments, be honest, and demonstrate that I'm doing my best to have a successful relationship."

"Good plan. Let's do that."

And there it is. High Trust happens when we earn it, and not because of a title, tenure, or role that we play. In fact, no one really cares about any of those things. But, that's only the beginning, and it's not quite that simple to do this at scale, because unlike interacting with a neighbor or a CTO, we need to generate trust on a large scale. And that requires purposeful *infrastructure*.

Needing More Time for Strategy

When I started Broadsword, I had already had some good experience as a leader and manager, but I had never led a company. Even though my experience informed me to self-organize rather than manage, I was caught up in HR, marketing, selling, and operations, and I was depending on the high performance of the team members I had known for years to do what was right for the company. Even though my own experience was as a servant leader who tried to create a model for self-organization, I assumed I needed to emulate the leaders from some of the large companies I had worked for, especially Ernst and Young, where all Senior Managers were given the book *Managing the Professional Services Firm* by David Maister (Simon & Schuster, 2007) as their guide. Maister's book called for "leverage," where a senior manager has several junior leaders reporting to him or her, and those junior leaders each have senior consultants, and those seniors have junior consultants, with each level managing the next. This model allowed the firm to maximize the knowledge and profitability of the senior manager – who ostensibly was the most experienced subject matter expert.

However, try as I might, my attempt at leverage, and to manage the company using traditional professional services management techniques failed. I tried to appoint managers, but few people followed their instructions. I tried to implement performance reviews, and the uber-high performing people I had hired didn't like it. I tried to implement team status meetings, and important team members didn't show. It was a disaster!

Then it struck me. I had done *too* good a job hiring people. I didn't hire the traditional leverage model, I hired an entire team of all-star performers. Thoroughbreds. Heroes. You can't manage them – you can only lead them. What an opportunity! That was the day we decided to eliminate all managers.

Over the next year, the company began to grow and get busier, and I became overwhelmed with mundane tasks. Every request was filtered through me, every major decision had to be made by me, and every problem had to be fixed by me. We were becoming more like a consortium, with each consultant running his or her own micro-business, with me serving as an information and decision-making hub. I no longer had time to set strategy, build infrastructure, think about training, and focus on other tasks that were about building value – I was treading water again. None of this was working for me, and we needed to do something different. That meant facing the music and starting with leadership. And that meant me.

Broadsword's Agile Transformation

Right out of the gate we decided to "use agile to be agile," and we spent time collaborating on our values, with me playing the role of Product Owner, and the team telling me what could be done, when it could be completed, and how much effort it would take. We adopted Trello as our standard, and developed multiple backlogs together that defined who we wanted to be in the future. We also identified some agile ceremonies we could start using right away, including a global daily stand-up that took place every day at 2:00 PM regardless of which state or country each consultant happened to be in. It was transformational. We also developed a performance model, the Agile Performance Holarchy, to assess our performance as we evolved and matured our agile culture.

We began by mind mapping the major components of the model that would be our baseline. Figure 73-1 depicts that model.

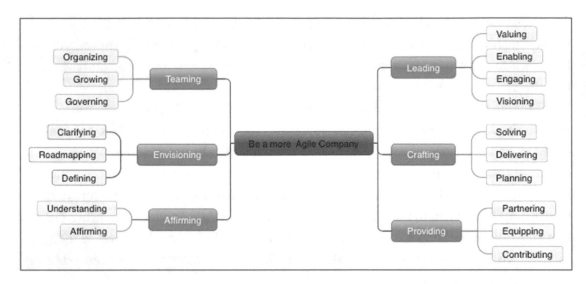

Figure 73-1. *Agile Performance Baseline*

We knew we had to start with Leadership and values, so in order to begin we established our Leading Objective in Epic format as:

Leading: *As an Agile Leader*
              I will project agile values, provide the environment, and establish a vision
              So that my teams can be agile and successful in everything they do.

Using the Story architecture depicted in the APH "Envisioning" Performance Circle, our Leading Epic was broken into four Leadership User Stories, one for each Holon within the Leadership Performance Circle:

Leading: Valuing   *As an Agile leaderI want to define, deploy, project and sustain agile valuesSo that many team understands the expectations for organizational agility.*

Leading: Engaging   *As an Agile "Servant Leader,I want to mentor and engage with agile teamsto ensure agile values are being embraced, and to remove impediments to their adoption.*

Leading: Envisioning *As an Agile LeaderI want to set and communicate a vision compatible with agile valuesSo that we can develop a healthy agile organization.*

Leading: Enabling   *As an Agile LeaderI want to design and deploy our set of Agile KeysSo our teams can understand what is required to advance our performance level.*

Writing user stories is nice, and they are perfect for getting at the meaning of the requirement, but as I've often said to the over two thousand students I've been lucky enough to teach, "nothing changes until someone does *something*." I started saying that as a reaction to the thousands of business meetings I've attended where people would talk *ad nauseum* about "what" someone else needed to do to make something happen, but rarely offered ideas on "how" the idea would come to fruition. We needed more detail to turn these ideas into reality, and to guide us in the future during times of stress. So we established a set of actions for all of the Performance Circles that described what it took to deliver the user stories for each Holon. The actions for the Leading Performance Circle are depicted in Figure 73-2.

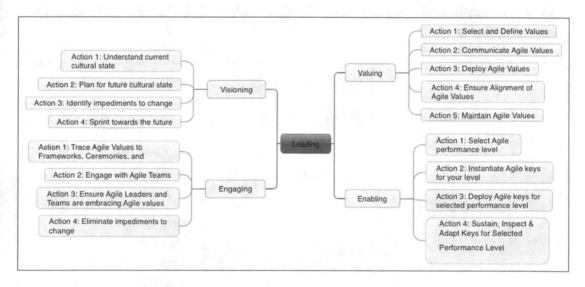

Figure 73-2. *Leading Performance Circle Actions*

Traditional leaders will note that it was the *team* that agreed to these Epics and User Stories. As the person who owned 100 percent of the stock in the company, I didn't *need* their agreement, but I knew that self-subscription was powerful, and it affected everything we did, and that meant transparency on everything, including my role, their roles, and the way we operated the company if we were ever going to have an agile culture. *Trust* is everything.

Transparency doesn't always mean agreement though. Sometimes leaders have roles that cannot be agreed to by the team. In fact, there are some things that all team members can't even *know* about, such as the results of performance reviews, and issues related to human resources, termination, legal, and taxation, but we can be transparent about what those things are, and why we need to keep them confidential within a smaller circle. Most of the time, the team gets it.

Leading: Valuing

As an Agile leader

I want to define, deploy, project and sustain agile values

So that many teams understand the expectations for organizational agility.

In order to complete our User Story on Valuing, we selected ceremonies and techniques depicted in Figure 73-3.

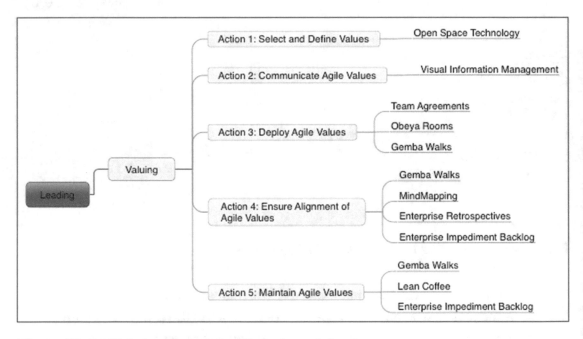

Figure 73-3. *Valuing Ceremony/Technique Selections*

Action 1: Select and Define Agile Values

Selected Ceremony/Technique:

1.   Open Space Technology

To address this Action as a team, we needed a transparent, safe, and structured collaborative ceremony. Sure, the agile values are known to all, but they're not universally understood and internalized, so conducting our first *Open Space* was a transformation event on our journey to agility. We chose to start with Open Space Technology because, we just weren't sure how we wanted to approach the objective.

Because we had never done this before, and we were determined to start off right, we engaged the master, Chris Sims from Agile Learning Labs. Chris, along with Hillary Louse Johnson, is the author of *The Elements of Scrum* (Dymaxicon, 2011), and had already trained our entire team in his engaging and practical Certified Scrum Master and Certified Scrum Product Owner classes. We were impressed with his philosophy and agile approach to business operations, and he was a perfect cultural fit for Broadsword.

Our first Open Space lasted one day together as a team, with a day of "theme" preparation, and some early morning setup, where Chris set up space throughout the hotel for people to "vote with their feet," and attend the sessions they were most interested in.

Many of our team members, who were ardent and experienced event planners, were pretty leery going into the Open Space, since there was no agenda, no pre-reading, and little planning for how the meeting would unfold. The fact that the event not only went splendidly, but also resulted in a common set of team values, as well as a plan to evolve into an agile organization, was enough to change our perspective on agile and self-organization. We were converts from that day on.

See Part 3 for more information on Open Space Technology (Chapter 41).

Action 2: Communicate Agile Values

Selected Ceremony/Technique:

1. Visual Information Management

Broadsword is a virtual company, and after 14 years of successful operations, we've never had an office other than "Broadsword HQ-North," a small 8' x 13' office in my home in southeastern Michigan. Things became even more complicated when we opened "Broadsword-HQ-South," an even smaller office in our Florida home, where we have been spending the winters since 2015.

Our team resides in Michigan (where we started), Florida, Maryland, California, and Massachusetts, with each team member flying close to two-hundred thousand miles per year. How do you openly share values, promote them every day, and ensure that the message is being delivered, with such a geographically dispersed organization?

Our solution to this Action was to implement the cloud-based, Bitrix24. Bitrix24 has all of the standard "professional services automation" tools, such as CRM, Workgroups, task tracking, calendar, artifact sharing, desktop sync, and two features that met our VIM needs: Workgroup-based wikis to share ad-hoc and unstructured workgroup/project information, and most importantly, a social media "wall," an intersection of Facebook and Twitter, that allows team members to not only see important information being posted about values, announcements, risks, or issues, but also post what they are thinking or doing at any given point in time. The tools also allow the creation and display of discussion threads, so all team members can weigh in on what's been posted. Bitrix24 runs on any device, and has the ability to "push" important messages to each team members by category, name, or job function.

See Part 3 for more information on Visual Information Management (Chapter 72).

Action 3: Deploy Agile Values

Selected Ceremonies/Techniques:

1.   Gemba Walks

2.   Team Agreements

3.   Obeya Rooms

As a result of our initial Open Space (we've done others since), Broadsword established our own team values, in addition to agile values, that defined us as a company. These include:

1.   Have the knowledge and content that our clients value.

2.   Have an established way of doing business.

3.   Be creative problem solvers focused on our clients.

4.   Understand our client's business and help them to be successful.

5.   Be professional and ethical at all times.

6.   Anticipate our client's needs.

7.   Be fun and hassle-free to work with.

In addition to our use of Visual Information Management and training for all team members in agile, scrum, and SAFe, we employ the Gemba Walks to regularly assess who were have become, and whether we like what we see in the mirror.

We've implemented virtual Obeya Rooms on our cloud-based collaboration tool that display our values, and we review them at every quarterly meeting, where we examine how well we are living up to them.

To further support agile values deployment, we have a team agreement, which gets reviewed by the entire team as a group at each quarterly meetup. Ideas, changes, and improvements are recorded in the Enterprise Impediment Backlog, and are used to address changes to the values, training, coaching, Performance Circles, Holons, Objectives, or Actions in the APH.

See Part 3 for more information on Obeya Rooms (Chapter 41), Gemba Walks (Chapter 31), and Team Agreements (Chapter 62).

Action 4: Ensure Alignment of Agile Values

Selected Ceremonies/Techniques:

1. Mind Mapping

2. Gemba Walks

3. Enterprise Retrospectives

4. Enterprise Impediment Backlog

Values are the bedrock of agile culture, but adopting them doesn't happen in a vacuum. They manifest themselves in the actions of leaders, team members, and customers, and must be traceable to every ceremony and technique used by every person, every day.

You've probably heard the terms "scrum-but," "agile-like," or "scrum-er-fall." These terms reflect a state of performance where the ceremonies and processes being adopted by teams and leaders are in conflict with Agile values, and are characterized by frustration and difficulty achieving success with Agile. Use of low-trust, command-and-control procedures, as defined in many Defined Process Control (DPC) models, too often at those companies attempting to implement CMMI and PMBOK, in an environment where teams are working to adopt agile values, can be toxic to the culture and create cynicism and resistance within the organization. There is nothing wrong with CMMI and PMBOK, and they can be quite powerful as a positive force for change, but there is a tendency to deploy them in a DPC, rather than Empirical Process Control (EPC) context, and that can be destructive to an Agile culture.

At one of our subsequent Open Spaces, we traced our values to each ceremony, technique or process used at Broadsword by creating mind maps using MindJet's MindManager, whereby we connected each of the agile values, and each of the Broadsword values, to the various ceremonies and techniques that we use in our company, ensuring that every one of them was in alignment and served the intention of the stated value.

Each time we run this exercise, we find new techniques that don't align quite how we would like them to, giving us new input into the Enterprise Impediment Backlog, a construct used to prioritize the improvements and changes to the system that will help make us more agile. This is our solution to "nothing changes until someone does something," and it becomes our to-do list.

See Part 3 for more information on Gemba Walks (Chapter 31), Enterprise Impediment Backlogs (Chapter 45), and Enterprise Retrospectives (Chapter 50).

Action 5: Maintain Agile Values

Selected Ceremonies/Techniques:

1. Lean Coffee – Values edition!

As leaders we do all we can to provide an environment for teams to collaborate, discuss, deploy, and maintain values, but it is the culture that maintains them and ensures that they are being demonstrated in everything we do. No matter what we, as leaders, do, we can't control it. We need the teams to control it – but that requires action.

Believing that culture happens on its own will only end in disappointment. Team members need to discuss it, improve it, and play an active role in shaping the company's culture. In order to encourage constructive but unstructured conversations about values, we encourage teams to engage in informal Lean Coffee events, where the agenda is set at the beginning by whomever shows up, and each topic is discussed for five minutes, with an additional five allocated if the team unanimously agreed.

These distributed, independent "mini-Open Space" events provide a powerful mechanism for strengthening the culture, and allow team members to feed the Enterprise Impediment Backlog without a manager present, often resulting in new and interesting ideas.

See Part 3 for more information on Lean Coffee (Chapter 38) and Enterprise Impediment Backlogs (Chapter 45).

Leading: Engaging

As an Agile "Servant Leader,"

I want to mentor and engage with agile teams

to ensure agile values of being embraced, and to remove impediments to their adoption.

In order to complete our User Story on Engaging, we selected the ceremonies and techniques depicted in Figure 73-4.

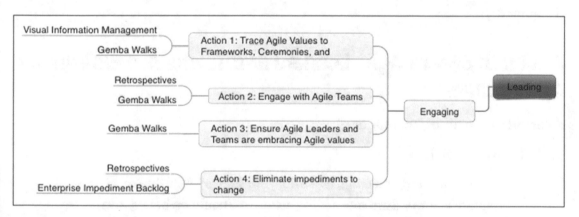

Figure 73-4. *Engaging Ceremony/Technique Selections*

Action 1: Trace Agile Values to Frameworks, Ceremonies, and Techniques

Selected Ceremonies/Techniques:

1.   Visual Information Management

2.   Gemba Walks

Using the Mind Maps created at our Open Space events, we communicate our values' traceability by posting them on our cloud-based wiki so all team members can view them and provide feedback.

See Part 3 for more information on Visual Information Management (Chapter 72) and Gemba Walks (Chapter 31).

Action 2: Engage with Agile Teams

Selected Ceremonies/Techniques:

1. Retrospectives

2. Gemba Walks

In addition to the retrospectives our team members conduct with their clients, we hold regular "account" retrospectives internally with our own team, where we discuss not only "what went well, what didn't, and what could be done differently," but also categorize and expand the retrospective to categorize it by operations, marketing, finance, client satisfaction, and, of course, the conduct of the project or engagement.

See Part 3 for more information on Retrospectives (Chapter 50) and Gemba Walks (Chapter 31).

Action 3: Ensure Agile Leaders and Teams Are Embracing Agile Values

Selected Ceremonies/Techniques:

1. Retrospectives

   At each quarterly meeting, we review the state of our values and explore where we are succeeding, where we could do better, and have an (often lively) debate about whether we should change or add to them.

2. Gemba Walks

   Regular visits to our clients and programs provide an opportunity to observe performance of our team members interacting with their clients, and they provide opportunities to evaluate alignment with agile values.

See Part 3 for more information on Retrospectives (Chapter 50) and Gemba Walks (Chapter 31).

Action 4: Eliminate Impediments to Change

Selected Ceremonies/Techniques:

1. Retrospectives

2. Enterprise Impediment Backlog

As Agile leaders, we often are called upon to act as enterprise scrum masters, tracking and removing the largest impediments prior to them becoming too large to easily remove. The use of the "operational retrospective," where team members come together inspect and examine how things are going – not only on their projects and client engagements, but within the context of business operations.

We've developed a semi-automated, anonymous version we call the "Team Happiness Circle" (Figure 73-5). Each week a large poster can be hung outside of a team room, and team members can mark how they are feeling in eight quadrants. This gives leaders instant information about how team members are feeling about each category.

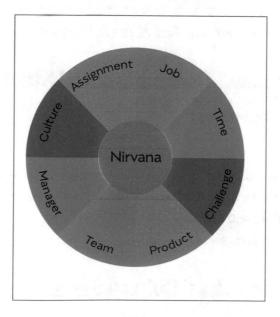

Figure 73-5. *The Team Happiness Circle*

See Part 3 for more information on Retrospectives (Chapter 50) and Enterprise Impediment Backlogs (Chapter 45).

Leading: Visioning

As an Agile Leader

I want to set and communicate a vision compatible with agile values

So that we can develop a healthy agile organization.

In order to complete our User Story on Visioning, we selected the ceremonies and techniques depicted in Figure 73-6.

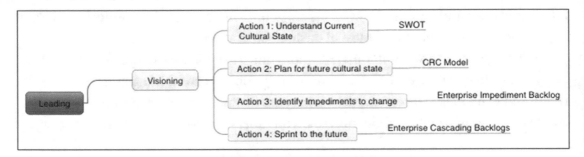

Figure 73-6. *Visioning Ceremony/Technique Selections*

Action 1: Understand Current Cultural State

Selected Ceremonies/Techniques:

1. SWOT

At each quarterly meeting, we apply SWOT, an analysis of strengths, weaknesses, opportunities, and threats with subcategories sometimes being examined to include sales, marketing, training, and more.

See Part 3 for more information on SWOT (Chapter 62).

Action 2: Plan for Future Culture State

Selected Ceremonies/Techniques:

1. CRC Model

CRC modeling, a technique typically applied in an object-oriented context, is ideal for modeling culture and performance with an agile organization, where linear procedure and hierarchies are minimized in favor of holarchies and empirical processing. We typically use Mind Mapping as a tool to model our organization and processes.

See Part 3 for more information on the CRC Model (Chapter 23).

Action 3: Identify Impediments to Change

Selected Ceremonies/Techniques:

1. Enterprise Impediment Backlog

At the organizational level, we have more impediments than we can solve in a short timebox, so they are prioritized and placed on a backlog, to be solved by team members as they become available. Team members have the authority to subscribe to, and complete, items on the EIB.

We use Trello, an Atlassian product, for our Enterprise Impediment Backlog.

See Part 3 for more information on Enterprise Impediment Backlog (Chapter 45).

Action 4: Sprint Toward the Future State

Selected Ceremonies/Techniques:

1. Enterprise Cascading Backlogs (ECB)

With multiple product lines, service groups, and tools, we now manage our long-term improvements and plans for the future using multiple, related, interconnected backlogs. Team members self-subscribe to stories in the ECB when they are not engaged in client work. No stories are assigned by me, and team members are authorized to take any action needed to close the story without asking permission from a manager.

See Part 3 for more information on Enterprise Cascading Backlogs (Chapter 45).

Leading: Enabling

As an Agile Leader

I want to design and deploy our set of Agile Keys

So our teams can understand what is required to advance our performance level.

In order to complete our User Story on Enabling, we selected the ceremonies and techniques depicted in Figure 73-7.

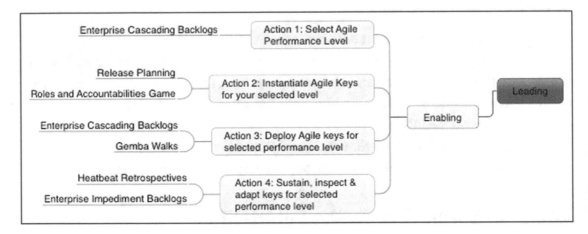

Figure 73-7. *Enabling Ceremony/Technique Selections*

Action 1: Select Agile Performance Level

Selected Ceremony/Technique:

1. Enterprise Cascading Backlogs

Agile Performance levels are defined by the Outcomes in each Holon within the APH. Our long-term plans are tied to the overall Performance Levels, with each Performance Circle capable of being assessed at Adopting, Transforming, or Mastering. With six Performance Circles, cascading backlogs can contain prioritized stories to achieve the highest level in each Circle over time.

See Part 3 for more information on Enterprise Cascading Backlogs (Chapter 45).

Action 2: Instantiate Agile Keys for Your Level

Selected Ceremonies/Techniques:

1. Release Planning

2. Roles and Accountabilities Game

Agile keys define the Roles, Ceremonies, and Actions that an organization selects in order to deploy agile behaviors within the organization. The most complex and difficult part of this for us was the shift from job titles and responsibilities, to roles and accountabilities.

Using the Roles and Accountabilities game, we collaborated on every possible role we could imagine within our company. These included roles like:

- Teacher of Classes

- Appraiser of Organizations

- Consultant to Clients

- Collector of Payments

- Writer of Proposals

- Seller of new work

- Depositor of money

- Scheduler of training

- Scheduler of consultants

- And more…

Roles were written on large sticky notes, and spread around the room on walls as column headers. When we were done, there were more than 40 roles covering two long walls.

Once we had agreement, each team member self-subscribed to the roles they felt they were best suited for by writing their name on the sticky note. Most team members had their name on more than one role, and many roles had multiple names tied to it.

Once the horse trading was over, and everyone was settled on their roles, each role owner went through process of establishing the accountabilities for each role, with accountabilities being defined as things they were authorized to do *without asking permission.*

For roles with one owner, this was a simple negotiation. They just had to make sure their accountabilities didn't trample on any others. For those where multiple people wore the same hat at least some of the time (such a "consultant to clients"), group collaboration was required.

The Roles and Accountabilities game is one of the most powerful ceremonies we've ever adopted. In one day, it provided us with the following benefits:

- Team members no longer felt the need to ask permission to act, freeing me up to focus on strategy.

- Our documented roles and accountabilities map clearly defined who was accountable for each action, eliminating dozens of phone calls and emails per month to work out the confusion.

- Posting the Roles and Accountabilities map in public eliminated confusion and reduced stress in the workplace.

- Provided an architecture for negotiating changes to roles and accountabilities among team members, enabling them to self-organize around what is best for the company.

See Part 3 for more information on Release Planning (Chapter 49) and the Roles and Accountabilities Game (Chapter 52).

Action 3: Deploy Agile Keys for Selected Performance Level

Selected Ceremonies/Techniques:

1. Enterprise Cascading Backlogs

2. Gemba Walks

See Part 3 for more information on Enterprise Cascading Backlogs (Chapter 45) and Gemba Walks (Chapter 31).

Action 4: Sustain, Inspect, and Adapt Keys for Selected Performance Level

Selected Ceremonies/Techniques:

1. Heartbeat Retrospectives

2. Enterprise Impediment Backlog

Heartbeat retrospectives usually occur outside the context of a project or engagement, and are timeboxed to 90 minutes, with a special focus on roles, accountabilities, and ceremony selection.

See Part 3 for more information on Retrospectives (Chapter 50) and Enterprise Impediment Backlogs (Chapter 45).

What's Next For You?

After you've worked through the Leadership Performance Circle, explore the remainder of the Agile Performance Holarchy to determine what applies to your organization, and what doesn't:

- **Leading** provides guidance to leaders on projecting agile values, and engaging with your teams in a more agile and self-organizing way.

- **Crafting** provides guidance for the design, development, and testing of products or services.

- **Providing** offers information on what it takes to provide an Agile infrastructure, including working with Agile suppliers.

- **Envisioning** addresses an architecture for defining great products and services.

- **Affirming** helps to evaluate the quality of team performance and products.

- **Teaming** provides guidance on governance and self-organization for Agile teams.

Tie the *Actions* within each Holon to the ceremonies and techniques your team has selected, in the same way Broadsword did as demonstrated above. If you are using alternative ceremonies to meet the intention of each action, that's great! Keep doing that, and work to make it better. If not, there are a host of suggestions in Section 3 of this book.

Finally, you can use the APH to assess your organization by using the *outcomes* identified within each Holon. The outcomes define a target for *adopting, transforming,* or *mastering* organizational agility, and provide a road map for moving to the next level within each Holon. A formal assessment could even result in an organizational Agile Performance certification with the APH.

If you are new to Agile leadership, and want to help your teams set a baseline for high performance, Part 3 is an illustrated guide to most common Agile ceremonies and techniques that will likely be used within your organization.

Both agile and organizational values should be traced to, and aligned with, every framework, ceremony, and technique that is adopted by the managers, supervisors, project managers, architects, DBAs, developers, analysts, tests, and process team members in your company to ensure that the actions on the ground accurately reflect the values agreed to by you and your team. This helps build an infrastructure for high trust, and makes adoption of agile simpler and more successful.

Remember – values lead to trust. And without trust there is no Agile. Trust is everything!

Good luck. And onward to Agility!

APPENDIX A

Quick Reference Tables

The following Tables A-1 through A-6 provide an "at a glance" reference to the Performance Circles, Holons, Objectives, Actions, Ceremonies, and Outcomes by Performance Level within the Agile Performance Holarchy. You can use these tables to quickly validate the approach being used by leaders and teams to enable high-performance agility.

© Jeff Dalton 2019

J. Dalton, *Great Big Agile*, https://doi.org/10.1007/978-1-4842-4206-3

Table A-1. Leading: "As an Agile Leader, I will project agile values, provide the environment, and establish a vision, so my teams can be agile and successful in everything they do"

HOLON	OBJECTIVE	ACTIONS	CEREMONIES/ TECHNIQUES	ROLES	ADOPTING OUTCOMES	TRANSFORMING OUTCOMES	MASTERING OUTCOMES
Valuing	As an agile leader, I want to define, deploy, project and sustain, agile values, so that my team understands the expectations for organizational agility.	Select and Define Agile Values	Open Space Technology, Brainstorming, Mind Mapping, Value Tracing, Big Room Planning	CxO(s) Agile Leaders Enterprise Scrum Masters	1. Agile values are selected and defined.	6. Essential stakeholders are engaged and demonstrate agile values.	9. Agile leaders at all levels are engaged in support of agile values.
		Communicate Agile Values	Obeya Rooms, Gemba Walks, Visual Information Management		2. Agile roles and accountabilities are defined.	7. Agile Leaders are trained to live and project agile values.	10. Visual information management techniques are used to display project agile values.
		Deploy Agile Values	Obeya Rooms, Gemba Walks, Team Chartering/ Team Agreements		3. Agile ceremonies and techniques are defined.	8. Agile values are prominently displayed throughout each facility.	11. Agile values are reevaluated, adjusted, and improved over time.
		Ensure alignment of Agile Values	Gemba Walks, Enterprise Retrospectives, Enterprise Impediment Backlog, Mindmapping		4. Agile teams are trained.		
		Maintain Agile Values	Gemba Walks, Lean Coffee, Enterprise Retrospectives, Enterprise Impediment Backlog		5. Agile teams self-subscribe to established values.		

Engaging	Trace agile values to frameworks, ceremonies, and techniques	Visual Information Management, Gemba Walks, Lean Coffee	CxO(s), Agile Leaders, Enterprise Scrum Masters	1. Agile values are traced to frameworks, ceremonies, and techniques.	3. Agile teams use defined frameworks, ceremonies, and techniques.	5. Leaders at all levels of the business use defined frameworks, ceremonies, and techniques in their everyday work.
As an agile "servant leader," I want to mentor and engage with Agile teams, to ensure agile values are being embraced and remove impediments to their adoption.	Engage with Agile teams	Visual Information Management, Gemba Walks, Retrospectives, Scrum of Scrums		2. Constraints and impediments are identified and eliminated.	4. Backlog that defines future state of performance is maintained.	
	Ensure Agile Leaders and teams are embracing Agile values	Visual Information Management, Gemba Walks, Retrospectives, Scrum of Scrums				
	Eliminate impediments to change	Retrospectives, Enterprise Impediment Backlog, Gemba Walks				

(continued)

Table A-1. (*continued*)

HOLON	OBJECTIVE	ACTIONS	CEREMONIES/ TECHNIQUES	ROLES	ADOPTING OUTCOMES	TRANSFORMING OUTCOMES	MASTERING OUTCOMES
Visioning	As an agile leader, I want to set and communicate a vision compatible with agile values, so that we can develop a healthy Agile organization.	Understand current cultural state Plan for future (or desired) cultural state Identify impediments to change Sprint toward the future state	SWOT CRC Model, SWOT SWOT, Enterprise Impediment Backlog Enterprise Cascading Backlogs, Enterprise Impediment Backlog	CxO(s) Agile Leaders Enterprise Scrum Masters	1. Current state of organizational performance is defined. 2. Future state is identified and displayed.	3. SWOT is completed and published. 4. Backlog to future state exists in visual format. 5. Culture transformation release plan exists.	6. Organizational performance sprints are executed. 7. Progress is visually displayed using visual information management. 8. Impediments to organizational performance are regularly identified and removed.

Enabling	As an agile leader, I want to design and deploy our set of Agile Keys, so that my teams understand what is required to advance our performance level.	Select Agile performance level	Enterprise Cascading Backlogs	CxO(s)	1. Agile performance levels are identified for each Holon.
		Instantiate Agile keys for your level	Enterprise Cascading Backlogs, Gemba Walks, Sprint Planning, Release Planning	Agile Leaders	2. Agile Keys for each level are used as is or customized for local context.
		Deploy Agile keys for selected performance level	Enterprise Cascading Backlogs, Gemba Walks	Enterprise Scrum Masters	3. Agile teams are trained on Agile Keys.
		Sustain, inspect, and adapt keys for selected performance level	Enterprise Cascading Backlogs, Enterprise Impediment Backlog, Heartbeat Retrospectives		4. Agile teams use Agile Keys to transform the way they work.
					5. Heartbeat Retrospectives are held.
					6. Improvements from retrospectives are implemented.

305

Table A-2. *Providing:* *"As an agile leader, I want to foster a continuous improvement environment and engage with agile partners, so that my agile teams can grow their capabilities"*

HOLON	OBJECTIVE	ACTIONS	CEREMONIES/ TECHNIQUES	ROLES	ADOPTING OUTCOMES	TRANSFORMING OUTCOMES	MASTERING OUTCOMES
Contributing	As an agile leader, I want to help teams identify, capture, and deploy lessons based on their experience, so that we can improve our performance.	Identify Best Practices Share and implement Best Practices Identify improvements Share and Implement Improvements	Retrospective, Enterprise Retrospective, Functional Retrospective Best Practices Board (or Wiki), Improvement Backlog Grooming Retrospective, Enterprise Retrospective Best Practices Board, Improvement Backlog Grooming	Scrum Master Team Members Agile Leader	1. Teams capture best practices for adoption. 2. Teams inspect and adapt performance. 3. Teams reflect on how to become more effective. 4. Improvements are adopted by projects.	5. Organizations capture enterprise-wide feedback. 6. Agile Leaders are trained in how to capture, select, and deploy improvements. 7. Best practices are leveraged across the organization. 8. Improvements are deployed across the organization.	9. Agile Leaders support enterprise-wide ceremonies that include teams, partners, and suppliers. 10. Agile leaders collaborate with internal and external stakeholders on improvements.

Partnering	As an agile leader, I want to define relationships and agreements between teams and internal/external partners and suppliers, so that I can extend the capabilities of my Agile teams.	Identify internal and external agile partners Assess Partner's Agile Capabilities Develop Agile partnering agreement Engage with partners using Agile Partnering Agreement	Envisioning Sprint, Project Chartering/Team Agreements, Release Planning Agile Partner Assessment Agile Partnering Agreement Stakeholder Identification and Management, Backlog Grooming, Sprint Planning, Release Planning, Acceptance Testing	Agile Leader Scrum Master CxO Team Members Procurement Department	1. Multiple potential Agile Partners identified. 2. Evaluation for the selection of agile partners was performed using criteria that maps to values. 3. Establish agreement with Partner that aligns with Agile frameworks, methods, and techniques. 4. Develop partner communication plan.	5. All key stakeholders are engaged with agile ceremonies. 6. Training provided for internal stakeholders on agreement and their alignment with agile values and methods. 7. Verify that agreement aligns with agile values and methods.	8. Partner evaluation survey performed post agreement, and incrementally throughout the program. 9. Preferred partners are established using data about their alignment with agile values and are known and understood to all teams. 10. Deploy agreements to all suppliers and partners that interact with delivery teams.

(continued)

Table A-2. (*continued*)

HOLON	OBJECTIVE	ACTIONS	CEREMONIES/ TECHNIQUES	ROLES	ADOPTING OUTCOMES	TRANSFORMING OUTCOMES	MASTERING OUTCOMES
Equipping	As an agile leader, I want to enable Agile teams by equipping them with co-located space, tools, and training, so that people have everything needed to succeed as a self-organizing team.	Acquire and set up space for teams Provide tools for teams to use Deliver training and mentoring	Team Room Set Up Meeting Envisioning Sprints, Brainstorming, Agile Partner Assessment Experiential Training, Classroom Training, E-learning, Coaching and Mentoring	Agile Leaders Agile Team Trainer / Coach	1. Teams have a dedicated working space that aligns with localized agile values. 2. Tools and automation are selected, identified, and available for team use. 3. Training is conducted that meets team's needs.	4. Team Space is set up in accordance with organization agile values. 5. Tools and automation meet the project team needs. 6. Training is conducted on organizational values and tools for all team members.	7. Agile leaders evaluate how team space and tools are working for team members. 8. Tools and automation are leveraged across all teams. 9. The agile organization supports learning as a core capability.

Table A-3. Envisioning: *"As a product owner, I will establish a roadmap, release plan, and backlog, so the overall vision of the product/service can be realized"*

HOLON	OBJECTIVE	ACTIONS	CEREMONIES/ TECHNIQUES	ROLES	ADOPTING OUTCOMES	TRANSFORMING OUTCOMES	MASTERING OUTCOMES
Road Mapping	As a product owner, I want to define a product road map and backlog, so that there are prioritized backlogs that define the product vision.	Identify current and future product capabilities	Big Room Planning, Open Spaces Technology, Research Competitors, Market Research, Customer Interviews, Product Comparisons	Product Owners, Product Management Teams, Subject Matter Experts, Agile Teams	1. Product vision reflects product needs and key functional/ nonfunctional attributes	4. Product vision reflects the target customers/ users.	8. Product vision and road map updated over time and consistently kept up to date.
		Create product vision	Envisioning Sprints, Product Scenarios, Prototyping, Kano Model		2. Product vision reflects product feasibility and key barriers	5. Product vision is compared against existing products for potential reusability.	9. Road-mapping ceremonies and techniques are improved and expanded over time.
		Create product road map	Envisioning Sprints, Product Scenarios, Prototyping, Kano Model		3. Road map aligns with product vision and describes product goals	6. Product vision reflects the product revenue model and value proposition.	
		Define and charter Agile teams	Project Chartering, Team Agreements			7. Road map aligns with product vision.	

(continued)

Table A-3. (*continued*)

HOLON	OBJECTIVE	ACTIONS	CEREMONIES/ TECHNIQUES	ROLES	ADOPTING OUTCOMES	TRANSFORMING OUTCOMES	MASTERING OUTCOMES
Defining	As a product owner, I want to define a product road map and backlog, so that there are prioritized backlogs that defines the product vision.	Allocate Road Map work for Agile teams	Backlog Grooming, Release Planning	Product Owners	1. Backlog reflecting product vision with features and capabilities exists.	4. Product owner engages with agile team in all product ceremonies.	8. Multiple product backlogs are synchronized across agile teams.
		Develop Road Map Product Backlog	Backlog Grooming, Release Planning, Three Diverse Humans	Product Management Teams	2. Product owners and agile team members are trained in the creation and management of the product backlog.	5. Prioritized and sized product backlog exists.	9. Product backlogs are updated, refined, and kept current at all times.
		Prioritize Road Map Product Backlog	Backlog Grooming, Release Planning	Scrum Masters	3. Cross-functional teams are effectively peer reviewing the backlog.	6. Product road map exists with epics allocated over time.	10. Release plan is updated, refined, and kept current at all times.
				Agile Teams		7. Release plan is visually available and understood by all team members.	11. Product definition ceremonies and techniques are improved and expanded over time.

310

Clarifying				
As a product owner, I want to transform customer needs from the product backlog into epics and user stories, so that agile teams can develop the product in an iterative and incremental fashion.	Evolve business needs into user and child stories Refine the product backlog Size the product backlog items	Backlog Grooming Backlog Grooming, Relative Estimation, Team Estimation Game, Release Planning	Product Owners Scrum Masters Agile Teams	1. Agile team members are trained in the development and analysis of user stories. 2. Product Backlog representing road map consists of epics and user stories.	3. Product Owner engages with Agile team during sprint planning, backlog grooming and sprint demos. 4. Product Backlog consists of epics and user stories that are prioritized, sized, and traced to test cases and changes.	5. All Product Owners engage with respective agile teams across the organization. 6. Product Backlog consists of epics, user stories, estimates, acceptance criteria, and definition of done. 7. Clarifying ceremonies and techniques are improved and expanded over time.

311

Table A-4. Crafting: "*As an agile Leader, I want agile team members engaged in the planning and building of high quality products, so that we deliver the solution as expected*"

HOLON	OBJECTIVE	ACTIONS	CEREMONIES/ TECHNIQUES	ROLES	ADOPTING OUTCOMES	TRANSFORMING OUTCOMES	MASTERING OUTCOMES
Planning	As an agile leader, I want agile team members to estimate and plan for the upcoming sprint and groom the backlog mid-sprint, so that we meet the sprint forecast as planned.	Enable Team commitment Create and agree on a Definition of Done Select work to complete in each sprint Estimate the work to be completed in the sprint	Project Chartering/ Team Agreement, Self-Subscription Project Chartering, Team Agreements, Definition of Done, Backlog Grooming Incremental Development, Definition of Ready, Self-Subscription Relative Estimation, Team Estimation Game, Backlog Grooming, Sprint Planning	Scrum Masters Product Owners Team Members	1. Projects demonstrate the use of established agile planning ceremonies and techniques. 2. Agile values are demonstrated during planning. 3. Project team members are trained in the agile planning ceremonies and techniques.	4. Essential planning stakeholders engage with projects while demonstrating agile values. 5. Agile leaders are trained in agile planning ceremonies and techniques and use them for their own work. 6. All projects and functional groups use agile planning ceremonies and techniques.	7. Projects select planning ceremonies and techniques based on project needs and objectives. 8. Agile leaders engage with projects using agile values. 9. Planning ceremonies and techniques are improved and expanded over time.

Solving	As an agile leader, I want to help agile team members meet their sprint forecast, so that we develop a high-quality solution using an iterative and incremental approach.	Burn down user stories	Burn Down Chart, Scrum Wall, Kanban Board, Velocity, Pair Programming, Mob Programming, Test-Driven Development, Unit Testing	Scrum Masters Product Owners Team Members	1. Teams use established development ceremonies and techniques.	4. Essential product development stakeholders demonstrate agile values.	7. Teams proactively select product development ceremonies and techniques and techniques based on project needs, objectives and constraints.
		Review activities and impediments	Daily Stand-Up, Impediment Backlog		2. Agile values are demonstrated during product development.	5. Agile Leaders are trained in how to recognize established product development ceremonies and techniques.	8. Agile leaders engage with teams using agile values.
		Remove Impediments	Impediment Backlog		3. Team members are trained in the established product development ceremonies and techniques	6. All teams in the organization select product development ceremonies and techniques	9. Product development ceremonies and techniques are improved and expanded over time.
		Review Completed Work	Sprint Demo				
		Identify Improvements	Sprint Retrospective, Milestone Retrospective				

(continued)

313

Table A-4. (*continued*)

HOLON	OBJECTIVE	ACTIONS	CEREMONIES/ TECHNIQUES	ROLES	ADOPTING OUTCOMES	TRANSFORMING OUTCOMES	MASTERING OUTCOMES
Delivering	As an agile leader, I want team members to integrate and test the solution, so that it meets the needs of the customer and end user.	Plan each Delivery Assemble product or service components for the sprint Test assembled product or service Deliver the assembled product or service	Release Planning, Backlog Grooming Automated Build, Continuous Integration Acceptance Testing, Usability Testing Continuous Deployment, Frequent Releases	Scrum Masters Product Owners Team Members	1. Projects use defined delivery ceremonies and techniques. 2. Agile values are demonstrated during delivery. 3. Project team members are trained in the defined delivery ceremonies and techniques.	4. Essential delivery stakeholders engage with projects using agile values. 5. Agile leaders are trained in the delivery ceremonies and techniques. 6. All projects use defined delivery ceremonies and techniques.	7. Projects proactively select organizational delivery ceremonies and techniques based on project needs, objectives, and constraints. 8. Agile leaders engage with projects using agile values. 9. Delivery ceremonies and techniques are improved and expanded over time.

Table A-5. *Affirming: "As an agile leader, I want to confirm that teams are demonstrating agile values, methods and techniques as expected, so that I can understand what is working well and what needs improvement"*

HOLON	OBJECTIVE	ACTIONS	CEREMONIES/ TECHNIQUES	ROLES	ADOPTING OUTCOMES	TRANSFORMING OUTCOMES	MASTERING OUTCOMES
Confirming	As an agile leader, I want to evaluate how well team members adhere to agile values, frameworks, and techniques, so that I can understand where there are opportunities to improve team performance.	Observe adoption of agile behaviors	Gemba Walk, Evaluation	CxO(s) Agile Leaders Agile Coaches	1. Agile coach is assigned to each agile team and functional area.	4. Leaders regularly observe teams and functional areas in person.	6. Coaches identify best practices and team improvements that can be shared across teams and functional areas.
		Gather information from agile teams about their adoption of agile techniques, behaviors	Gemba Walk, Evaluation, Review, Kamishibai Board	CxO(s) Agile Leaders Agile Coaches	2. Coaches are regularly observing and evaluating agile teams and functional areas.	5. Teams and functional areas identify and implement performance improvements based on the feedback they receive from coaches and leaders.	7. Enterprise retrospectives utilize feedback from coaches and leaders to improve performance across teams and functional areas.
		Provide improvement feedback to agile teams	Gemba Walk, Evaluation, Review, Kamishibai Board	Agile Leaders Agile Coaches	3. Coaches are regularly providing feedback to agile teams, leaders, and functional areas.		8. Leaders use data to confirm that their teams and functional areas are adopting agile values and techniques.
		Use improvement feedback to improve agile team performance	Gemba Walk, Evaluation, Review, Kamishibai Board	Agile Leaders Agile Coaches Agile Teams			

(continued)

Table A-5. (*continued*)

HOLON	OBJECTIVE	ACTIONS	CEREMONIES/TECHNIQUES	ROLES	ADOPTING OUTCOMES	TRANSFORMING OUTCOMES	MASTERING OUTCOMES
Understanding	As an agile leader, I want to know if we are receiving the benefits of agile adoption, so that the business can understand its performance and find ways to improve.	Identify metrics to understand project, product, team, and process performance	Goal, Question, Metric (GQM), Visual Information Management, Retrospectives, Lean Coffee	CxO(s) Agile Leaders Scrum Masters	1. Agile teams are collecting basic velocity metrics to understand their performance.	6. Teams adopt a shared set of organizational metrics that are used to understand their collective performance.	9. Performance metrics from teams and functional areas are aggregated and trended to understand organizational performance.
		Collect and report metrics data	Visual Information Management, Retrospectives, Scrum of Scrums	Agile Leaders Scrum Masters	2. Agile Teams are collecting basic metrics to understand the quality of the products they are developing.	7. Teams adopt a shared set of organizational metrics that are used to understand the quality of the products they are developing.	10. Product quality metrics from agile teams are aggregated and trended to understand organizational product quality.
		Analyze and trend metrics data	Evaluation, Visual Information Management, Retrospectives, Review	CxO(s) Agile Leaders Scrum Masters	3. Agile metrics are visually displayed. 4. Agile metrics are reviewed regularly by the team.	8. Metrics are utilized and reviewed during agile ceremonies (e.g., Sprint Planning, Retrospectives,	11. Agile teams are using metrics to improve performance and quality.
		Identify actions to improve performance	Evaluation, Visual Information Management, Retrospectives, Review	CxO(s) Agile Leaders Scrum Masters	5. Teams are meeting to discuss outcomes and solve problems		12. The organization is using metrics to improve performance and quality.

Table A-6. *Teaming:* *"As an agile leader, I want teams and functional areas to learn and master self-organization and agile ceremonies and techniques, so that the entire organization can benefit fully from agile adoption"*

HOLON	OBJECTIVE	ACTIONS	CEREMONIES/ TECHNIQUES	ROLES	ADOPTING OUTCOMES	TRANSFORMING OUTCOMES	MASTERING OUTCOMES
Organizing	As an agile leader, I want to support an agile infrastructure of people, processes, and tools, so that agile teams have everything needed to be successful.	Establish agile team environments Establish roles and accountabilities Promote self-organizing and cross-functional teams	Agile Digs Roles and Accountabilities Game Shared Vision (Obeya Room), Gemba, Kaizen	Agile Leaders Scrum Teams Scrum Masters	1. Physical space and culture is conducive to team collaboration, communication, and focus. 2. Teams have the right mix of cross-functional experience necessary to support agile development. 3. Teams establish standards and ground rules. 4. Teams clearly establish roles and accountabilities.	5. Teams establish charters consistent with the culture and values of the agile organization. 6. Ceremonies and techniques are available to all projects. 7. Teams begin to own their agile environment. 8. Team environments reflect agile values.	9. Teams self-organize based on the organizational agile culture defined and leaders can measure performance. 10. Projects optimize performance using accessible tools and techniques that are visible organizationally. 11. Agile teams integrate or synchronize with other teams and groups as needed to become a Team of Teams.

(*continued*)

Table A-6. (*continued*)

HOLON	OBJECTIVE	ACTIONS	CEREMONIES/ TECHNIQUES	ROLES	ADOPTING OUTCOMES	TRANSFORMING OUTCOMES	MASTERING OUTCOMES
Growing	As an agile leader, I want to provide a training, mentoring, and learning environment, so that teams can take full advantage of agile ceremonies, methods, and techniques.	Identify training needs for agile teams	Dot Voting	Agile Leaders Agile Teams Scrum Coach	1. Immediate and future training needs are identified.	4. Team effectiveness is measured.	7. Learning is based on team effectiveness measures.
		Develop an organizational training backlog	Product Training Backlog		2. Teams regularly review training status.	5. Training is visible in the team environment.	8. Training is constant, consistent, and readily available.
		Establish a mentoring program	Arc of Conversation		3. Trained mentors are present to increase team performance.	6. Teams determine training needs.	9. Team member competency is evident and demonstrable.
		Assess the effectiveness of training and mentoring programs	Confirmation Retrospectives, Training Retrospectives				

Governing				Agile Leaders	
As an agile leader, I want to provide a strong agile governance infrastructure for both product and process performance, so that as the business changes, our Agile values remain in alignment.	Align HR with requirements for self-organizing teams	Organizational Roles and Accountabilities Game		Enterprise Scrum Masters	1. Agile roles and accountabilities are understood by team members.
	Clarify team structure and reporting relationships	State of the Team		Agile Teams	2. Teams identify improvement opportunities.
	Empower a cross-functional group to deliver continuous performance improvement	All Hands Raised			3. Agile leaders and team members understand agile values.
	Assess internal initiatives to ensure that they align with the Agile values and future state	Retrospectives, Gemba Walks			4. Team members share roles and accountabilities when needed.
					5. Team outputs inform performance and organizational improvements.
					6. Team objectives and key results are assessed for alignment with agile values.
					7. Roles and accountabilities are flexible to meet current team needs.
					8. Agile leaders and development team members collaborate to drive continuous improvement.
					9. Agile teams are self-governing and agile leaders encourage and support team governance structures.
					10. Team objectives and key results are aligned with core organization-wide agile values.

319

Glossary

Acronyms

3Cs	Card, Conversation, and Confirmation
APH	Agile Performance Holarchy
APHAM	Agile Performance Holarchy Assessment Method
API	Application Programming Interface
AS9100	A company-level certification based on a standard published by the Society of Automotive Engineers (SAE) titled "Quality Systems-Aerospace-Model for Quality Assurance in Design, Development, Production, Installation and Servicing." The standard is based on organizational processes and emphasizes the need to satisfy internal, governmental, and regulatory requirements.
BDD	Business-Driven Development
BRP	Big Room Planning
CI	Continuous Integration
CMM	Capability Maturity Model
CMMI	Capablity Maturity Model Integration. A process model developed by the Software Engineering Institute and CMMI Institute that provided "what-a-bility" guidance to organizations who wish to improve performance.
CRC Cards	Class, Responsibilities, and Collaborators
DOD	Definition Of Done
DOR	Definition of Ready/Ready for Work
DPC	Defined Process Control
DO-178B	A standard for safety-critical software used in airborne systems

(*continued*)

© Jeff Dalton 2019
J. Dalton, *Great Big Agile*, https://doi.org/10.1007/978-1-4842-4206-3

EPC	Empirical Process Control
GQM	Goal Question Metric
GQIM	Goal Question Indicator Metric
INVEST	Independent, Negotiable, Valuable, Estimable, Sized, and Testable
ISO 9001	A standard published by the International Organization for Standardization that specifies requirements for a quality management system. Organizations use the standard to demonstrate the ability to consistently provide products and services that meet customer and regulatory requirements.
LMS	Learning Management System
ORA	Organizational Roles and Accountabilities
ORR	Organizational Roles and Responsibilities
PMBOK	Project Management Body of Knowledge
SLA	Service Level Agreement
SME	Subject Matter Expert
SWOT	Strengths Weaknesses Opportunities Threats
TDD	Test-Driven Development
TDH	Three Diverse Humans
UAT	User Acceptance Testing
VIM	Visual Information Management
XP	Extreme Programming

Terms

Action – The specific behavior that is applied to meet one of the APH Objectives. Agile ceremonies and techniques are performed to meet the intent of defined actions in the APH.

Adopting – The first of three APH Performance Levels that describe an organization's state of agile performance. Organizations that achieve this level of performance must demonstrate the Agile Keys and the Adopting Level Outcomes defined in the APH for one or more Holons.

Affirming – One of six performance circles in the APH. The Affirming performance circle describes the actions, roles, and outcomes that address the measurement and observation of team performance for the purpose of assessing agile adoption and enabling improvement. The Affirming performance circle has two Holons: Confirming and Understanding.

AgileCxO – The organization that owns the APH and the APHAM and provides certifications to agile organizations that have achieved an APH Performance Level. The term "CxO" stands for a corporate executive leader such as the Chief Executive Officer, Chief Operating Officer, or Chief Technology Officer.

Agile Coach – *See* Coach.

Agile Leader – The person who leads one or more agile teams or groups by defining and deploying agile values, providing an enabling infrastructure, developing an organizational vision for agility, and modeling agile values.

Agile Keys – The APH contains three Agile Keys that are instantiated for each APH Holon:

- Key 1: Defined Roles

- Key 2: Defined Ceremonies and Techniques

- Key 3: Actions

Verification of the Agile Keys is required to achieve an APH Performance Level.

Agile Manifesto – A collection of 12 guiding principles for improving the quality and experience of software product development.

Agile Partner – An individual or group that enters into an agile partnering agreement with an agile team or organization to extend the capabilities of the team/organization. An Agile Partner may be an internal department or employee or an external company or contractor.

Agile Performance Holarchy – A how-ability model that provides agile leaders and teams with an operating system to build, evaluate, and sustain great agile habits and behaviors. Components of the APH include: Performance Circles, Holons, Objectives, Actions, and Ceremonies/Techniques.

Agile Supplier – An external company or individual that works with an agile team or organization to deliver products and/or services defined in an agile agreement or contract.

Agile Team – A small group of co-located people who have shared accountability to achieve a goal and operate using agile methods, ceremonies and techniques. Also known as the Development Team.

Analyst – A role that conducts analysis as part of a user story and design validation technique known as Three Diverse Humans.

APHAM Assessment – An evaluation of organizational agile performance conducted by a Certified APH Assessor for the purpose of achieving certification in the Agile Performance Holarchy and identifying improvement opportunities.

APH Performance Level – APH Performance Levels are: Adopting, Transforming, and Mastering.

AS9100 – A company-level certification based on a standard published by the Society of Automotive Engineers (SAE) titled "Quality Systems-Aerospace-Model for Quality Assurance in Design, Development, Production, Installation and Servicing." The standard is based on organizational processes and emphasizes the need to satisfy internal, governmental, and regulatory requirements.

Backlog – A list of epics and user stories that defines the work to be accomplished by an agile team. Common backlogs used by agile teams include: Product Backlog, Sprint Backlog, Impediment Backlog, Improvement Backlog, Training Backlog, and Enterprise Cascading Backlogs.

Business Customer – *See* Customer.

Business SME – *See* Subject Matter Expert.

Ceremony – Intentional actions that are performed at defined times; demonstrates desired behavior and meets the intent of an Action in the APH. *See also* Technique.

Chief Engineer – A role that is typically performed by a senior person and is responsible for an engineering department or organization and the engineering practices and tools used therein.

Child Story – A user story that is related to another "parent" user story and is typically smaller in size than the parent story. *See* User Story.

Clarifying – A holon within the Envisioning performance circle that describes a set of actions, outcomes, ceremonies and techniques required to iteratively evolve the business needs into **user** stories, child stories, and tasks and to better understand the customer's needs.

Coach – A person who helps an individual or a team to adopt and improve a method, ceremony, or technique.

Coachee – A recipient of coaching who benefits from learning and/or improving a method, ceremony, or technique.

Configuration Manager – A role that is responsible for the product configuration management strategy and tools for a team or organization.

Confirming – A holon within the Affirming performance circle that describes a set of actions, outcomes, ceremonies and techniques required to understand how agile behaviors have been adopted by the team and to improve team performance.

Contributing – A holon within the Providing performance circle that describes a set of actions, outcomes, ceremonies and techniques required to identify, capture, and deploy lessons based on the empirical experience of agile teams.

Crafting – One of six performance circles in the APH. The Crafting performance circle describes the actions, roles, and outcomes that address the capability lift and craftsmanship required to consistently deliver high-quality products and services. The Crafting performance circle has three Holons: Planning, Solving, and Delivering.

Customer – An individual or group that commissions an agile team to deliver a product or service. The customer is typically the entity that is purchasing the product or service.

Defining – A holon within the Envisioning performance circle that describes a set of actions, outcomes, ceremonies and techniques required to build the product backlog that defines the product vision and road map.

Delivering – A holon within the Crafting performance circle that describes a set of actions, outcomes, ceremonies and techniques needed to plan for product or service releases, assemble the product, test the product, and deliver the product or service to the customer or end user.

Developer – A role that is responsible for designing, developing, and testing a product. A developer may be a member of an Agile Team.

Enabling – A holon within the Leading performance circle that describes a set of actions, outcomes, ceremonies and techniques that will help leaders design and deploy the set of "Agile Keys" that define the APH performance levels of Adopting, Transforming, and Mastering.

End User – A person who uses a product in their native environment.

Engaging – A holon within the Leading performance circle that describes a set of actions, outcomes, ceremonies and techniques that will help leaders develop "servant leader" competencies to engage, mentor, and participate with the organization's agile community.

Envisioning – One of six performance circles in the APH. The Envisioning performance circle describes the actions, roles, and outcomes that address the architecture required to define high-quality products and services. The Envisioning performance circle has three Holons: Defining, Clarifying, and Road Mapping.

Equipping – A holon within the Providing performance circle that describes a set of actions, outcomes, ceremonies and techniques required to set up team space and equip the team with the tools to enable them to be an effective and successful self-organizing team.

Evaluator – A role that is responsible for performing an objective evaluation of an agile team to understand how work is being done. An evaluator typically baselines the agile team's performance against a defined standard.

Extended Team Member – A person who participates in some team activities and is not a core member of the agile team. This person may represent a function or a group that interfaces with the team for a specific purpose.

Functional Group – A group of people in an organization that perform a similar function (e.g., human resources, accounting).

Functional Group Member – A person who belongs to a functional group. *See also* Functional Group.

Functional Team – *See* Functional Group

Governing – A holon within the Teaming performance circle that describes a set of actions, outcomes, ceremonies and techniques required to provide a strong agile governance infrastructure for both product and process performance.

Growing – A holon within the Teaming performance circle that describes a set of actions, outcomes, ceremonies and techniques required to provide a training, mentoring, and learning environment.

Holon – A component of the APH that represents a set of actions and outcomes that can effectively stand alone, but are also part of a greater whole. There are 18 Holons in the APH.

How-ability Model – The set of behaviors, actions, and outcomes that help define and evaluate organizational success, and support the culture, goals, and objectives of the organization. This model answers the question, "How do we behave?"

ISO 9001 – A standard published by the International Organization for Standardization that specifies requirements for a quality management system. Organizations use the standard to demonstrate the ability to consistently provide products and services that meet customer and regulatory requirements.

Leading – One of six performance circles in the APH. The Leading performance circle describes the actions, roles, and outcomes for agile leaders to define and deploy agile values, provide an enabling infrastructure, develop an organizational vision for agility, and model agile values. The Leading performance circle has four Holons: Enabling, Valuing, Visioning, and Engaging.

Mastering – The third of three APH Performance Levels that describe an organization's state of agile performance. Organizations that achieve this level of performance must demonstrate the Agile Keys and the Mastering Level Outcomes defined in the APH for one or more Holons.

Objective – Each holon in the APH has one or more objectives that must be met in order to instantiate the value of the holon.

Organization – A structured group of people who work together and share a common purpose and set of values.

Organizational Type Mismatch – A situation that results in organizations that have leaders who desire agility but continue to apply a low-trust Defined Process Control model to run the business when a high-trust Empirical Process Control model is required.

Organizing – A holon within the Teaming performance circle that describes a set of actions, outcomes, ceremonies and techniques required to implement self-organization, interface with non-agile teams, and define the roles of project managers, product owners, and other roles not defined by any agile framework.

Outcome – Each holon in the APH contains a set of outcomes that can be used to evaluate, improve, and sustain high performance. The outcomes are categorized into three APH Performance Levels: Adopting, Transforming, and Mastering.

Partnering – A holon within the Providing performance circle that describes a set of actions, outcomes, ceremonies and techniques required to define relationships and agreements between teams and internal or external partners and suppliers.

Performance Circle – A component of the APH that encapsulates a discrete set of behaviors, with a unique set of interrelated actions and outcomes that are essential to successfully adopting, transforming, and mastering large-scale agile performance. There are six Performance Circles in the APH.

Performance Level – *See* APH Performance Level.

Planning – A holon within the Crafting performance circle that describes a set of actions, outcomes, ceremonies and techniques required to estimate and plan for the upcoming sprint or iteration, grooming the backlog, demonstrating successes, and inspecting and adapting team performance.

Product Owner – A role performed by a customer or end-user representative that is responsible for maximizing the value of the product developed by the agile team. The Product Owner manages the Product Backlog and collaborates with the agile team to ensure they understand backlog items and their priority. The Product Owner evaluates and accepts user stories after the agile team demonstrates them.

Product Management Team – A team or group that is accountable for one or more products and is responsible for planning, forecasting, producing, and marketing the product(s).

Program Manager – A role that is responsible for providing governance and oversight for two or more projects. *See also* Project Manager.

Program Sponsor – A role that is accountable for the success of a program (or project). A Program Sponsor is responsible for obtaining buy-in and involvement from stakeholders, supporting the Program Manager(s), and solving any problems that may impede the success of the program.

Project Manager – A role that is responsible for planning and executing a project or other initiative that has a defined scope, start date, and finish date.

Providing – One of six performance circles in the APH. The Providing performance circle describes the actions, roles, and outcomes related to providing an agile infrastructure that includes appropriate teams, partners, training, mentoring, and tools. The Providing performance circle has three Holons: Partnering, Contributing, and Equipping.

Road Mapping – A holon within the Envisioning performance circle that describes a set of actions, outcomes, ceremonies and techniques required to create the product vision, define the product road map based on the vision, and identify the resources needed to make the product a reality.

Scrum Master – A role performed by a member of the agile team that is responsible for facilitating the team's agile ceremonies, removing impediments that prevent the team from achieving its goals, and interacting with stakeholders outside the agile team on the team's behalf.

Self-Organizing – A behavior practiced by agile teams that is traceable to the agile values of high-trust and transparency. Self-organizing teams do not need a manager to assign them tasks. Work is assigned to the whole agile team, and each team member selects the tasks that they will complete. Tasks are prioritized and reviewed daily to ensure that all work is completed.

Software Architect – A role that is typically performed by an expert and is responsible for the technology choices, design, and technical direction for product development.

Software Developer – *See* Developer.

Solving – A holon within the Crafting performance circle that describes a set of actions, outcomes, ceremonies and techniques needed to create and sustain high-quality products and services from the viewpoint of the customer.

Stakeholder – An individual or group that is impacted by or accountable for the outcome of a project or other endeavor.

Story – *See* User Story or Child Story.

Subject Matter Expert (SME) – An individual or group that is a respected authority in one or more areas of expertise.

Teaming – One of six performance circles in the APH. The Teaming performance circle describes the actions, roles, and outcomes that address establishing and sustaining agile teams that are self-organized and high performing. The Teaming performance circle has three Holons: Organizing, Growing, and Governing.

Team Leader – The leader of one or more teams who defines the team's mission, establishes the team's membership, and provides the team with the required resources. *See also* Agile Leader.

Team Member – A person who belongs to a team. *See also* Agile Team.

Technique – Intentional actions performed with skill; demonstrates desired behavior and meets the intent of an Action in the APH. *See also* Ceremony.

Tester – A role that is responsible for verifying and/or validating the functionality, quality, and performance of a product. A tester may also participate in user story and design validation.

Trainer – A role that is responsible for providing education and/or instruction for the purpose of equipping a trainee to effectively apply the learning.

Transforming – The second of three APH Performance Levels that describe an organization's state of agile performance. Organizations that achieve this level of performance must demonstrate the Agile Keys and the Transforming Level Outcomes defined in the APH for one or more Holons.

Understanding – A holon within the Affirming performance circle that describes a set of actions, outcomes, ceremonies and techniques required to collect and analyze metrics in order to understand team and organizational performance and agility.

User Story – Increments of work identified by the Product Owner to be completed by an Agile Team. Each story contributes to the business value to be delivered by the agile team. Stories contain a role, goal, and a benefit and are recorded on cards, sticky notes, or in a tool like Trello or Jira.

Valuing – A holon within the Leading performance circle that describes a set of actions, outcomes, ceremonies and techniques that will help leaders define, deploy, project, and sustain agile values.

Visioning – A holon within the Leading performance circle that describes a set of actions, outcomes, ceremonies and techniques that will help leaders set and communicate a vision that is compatible with agile values and a healthy agile organization.

What-ability Model – The set of frameworks, methods, roles, and artifacts derived from industry-standard models or internal methodologies. This model answers the question, "What do we need to do?"

Why-ability Model – The set of values and guiding principles that are traced directly to the goals and methods of the organization. This model answers the question, "Why are we doing this?"

Index

A

Acceptance testing/user acceptance testing (UAT), 45, 84, 111–112, 127, 159, 322

Affirming
  ceremonies/techniques
    evaluation, 89, 90, 93–95, 315
    gemba walk, 93–95, 315
    goal, question, metric (GQM), 88
    kamishibai board, 93–95, 315
    lean coffee, 88, 316
    retrospectives, 88–91, 316, 318
    review, 88–91, 93–95, 315, 316
    scrum of scrums, 89, 316
    visual information
      management, 88–91, 316
  holon: confirming, 91–95
  holon: understanding, 86–91

Agile agreement, 113–115, 120, 323

Agile digs, 100, 117–118, 259

Agile frameworks
  how-ability models, 9, 326
  what-ability models, 9, 330
  why-ability models, 9, 330

Agile partner assessment, 44, 52, 119–120

Agile Performance Holarchy
  action, 12, 16, 289, 301, 322, 323
  ceremonies/technique, 12, 15, 16, 301, 322–324

holons, 10, 11, 14, 15, 284, 289, 296, 300, 322, 323, 325–327
objective, 17, 289, 301, 322, 323, 327
performance circles, 10, 12–14, 21, 22, 284, 289, 299, 323, 325–329

All Hands Raised, 108, 121–122

Arc of conversation, 104, 123–125

Automated build, 6, 83, 84, 127–128

B

Backlog grooming, 45, 48, 49, 58, 59, 66, 67, 73, 75, 82, 83, 129–131, 147, 159, 168, 205, 207, 217, 234, 235, 237, 255, 266

Best Practices Board, 48, 49, 133–134

Big Room Planning/Release Zero, 25, 61, 62, 135–137, 321

Brainstorming, 25, 52, 139–141

Burn down chart, 77–78, 143–145

C

Class, Responsibilities, Collaborators (CRC), 35, 36, 153–154, 294, 321

Confirmation, 104, 147–148, 221, 321

Continuous deployment, 84, 149–150, 171

Continuous integration (CI), 83, 127, 149, 151–152, 321